Patterns of Decay
Shakespeare's Early Histories

Patterns of Decay
Shakespeare's Early Histories

Edward I. Berry

University Press of Virginia
Charlottesville

THE UNIVERSITY PRESS OF VIRGINIA
Copyright© 1975 by the Rector and Visitors
of the University of Virginia

First published 1975

Library of Congress Cataloging in Publication Data
Berry, Edward I
　Paterns of decay.

　　Includes index.
　　1. Shakespeare, William, 1564-1616—Histories.
2. Shakespeare, William, 1564-1616—Criticism and interpretation.
I. Title.　PR2982.B47　822.3'3　74-32400　ISBN 0-8139-0595-8

Printed in the United States of America

To Margaret

Contents

Preface   ix

1 Henry VI: Chivalry and Ceremony   1
2 Henry VI: Justice and Law   29
3 Henry VI: Kinship   53
Richard III: The Self Alone   75
The Later Histories: From History to Character   104

Index   129

Preface

This study presents an extended argument for the dramatic integrity of Shakespeare's *Henry VI-Richard III* sequence and its consequently unique position among the English histories. The focus is upon an underlying conception of historical process that provides each work with a thematic center and binds together the entire series. In my analysis of each play I concentrate upon a dominant theme, expressed not only in language but in character and action, which both unifies the play and defines a single stage in the process of social and political disintegration depicted by the series as a whole. A final chapter traces the development away from history toward politics and personality that characterizes the histories from *King John* to *Henry V* and anticipates the concerns of the major tragedies. Without, I hope, exaggerating the merits of what are probably Shakespeare's earliest plays, I have tried to show that they dramatize singly and collectively a more coherent and compelling vision of historical experience than has been hitherto recognized.

Until rather recently scholarship on the *Henry VI* plays has been dominated by bibliographical questions that continue to evade definitive answers. The authorship of the plays, their dates and order of composition, have all been debated at length.[1] Throughout my discussion I assume that the entire tetralogy was written by Shakespeare in its natural order sometime during 1590-93; although I can claim no certainty for these opinions, they are shared, I believe, by a majority of contemporary editors and critics of the plays. I assume as well, though this matter has not been generally explored, that the completed series was

---

[1] See particularly Edmond Malone, "A Dissertation on the Three Parts of *King Henry VI*," in *The Plays and Poems of William Shakespeare by the Late Edmond Malone*, ed. James Boswell (London, 1821) XVIII; Madeleine Doran, Henry VI, Parts II *and* III: *Their Relation to* The Contention *and* The True Tragedy (Iowa City, Iowa, 1928); Peter Alexander, *Shakespeare's* Henry VI *and* Richard III (Cambridge, 1929); Leo Kirschbaum, "The Authorship of *1 Henry VI*," *PMLA*, 67 (1952), 809-22. For useful summaries of the issues and additional arguments, see the introductions to the *Henry VI* plays provided by John Dover Wilson for The New Cambridge Shakespeare and Andrew S. Cairncross for The New Arden Shakespeare.

performed whenever possible on successive days. That two-part plays were customarily presented in this manner is clear from the records of Henslowe's diary.[2]

My acknowledgments must begin with Jonas Barish and Stephen Orgel, who aroused my interest in the English histories and supported my graduate studies at the University of California, Berkeley, in ways too numerous to mention. At the University of Virginia I have benefited from the intellectual vitality of many colleagues, particularly Leopold Damrosch, Alan Howard, and William Kerrigan; I owe a special debt to Richard Waswo, whose keenness of wit has exhausted and encouraged me at every phase of this project. Lester Beaurline and Arthur Kirsch read the manuscript and offered useful suggestions. I am also grateful to my students of Shakespeare, whose curiosity about the early histories so often whetted my own; Robert Schwartz deserves special thanks for his help in preparing the manuscript for publication. During the course of this study I have been aided by grants from the University of Virginia and the National Endowment for the Humanities.

Charlottesville, Virginia
December 1974

[2] See, for example, the entries for *1* and *2 Tamburlaine, 1* and *2 Tambercam*, and *1* and *2 Hercules* in *Henslowe's Diary*, ed. R. A. Foakes and R. T. Rickert (Cambridge, 1961), pp. 26-34.

Patterns of Decay
Shakespeare's Early Histories

As fester'd members rot but by degree
Till bones and flesh and sinews fall away,
So will this base and envious discord breed.

1 Henry VI III.i.192-94

1 *Henry VI:* Chivalry and Ceremony

In Act II of *1 Henry VI* the warrior Talbot, having just retaken Orleans, accepts a courtly invitation to visit the Countess of Auvergne. The audience is informed that the Countess plans to capture Talbot, but the hero himself arrives at her castle apparently ignorant of her intentions. Upon Talbot's entrance the Countess at first marvels in disbelief that this "weak and writhled shrimp" (II.iii.22) could be the reputed "Scourge of France" (l. 14). Once convinced of his identity, however, she triumphantly proclaims him her prisoner. Talbot responds with laughter and a riddling retort, and within moments he has blown his horn and called in his waiting troops. Though tactically outmaneuvered, the Countess recovers her poise with aristocratic aplomb: begging forgiveness for her lack of hospitality, she expresses her admiration for Talbot and graciously agrees to entertain him and his troops with "cates" and wine. At this point the scene ends, and the Countess is never heard of again.

The Countess of Auvergne episode poses the traditional question of the unity of *1 Henry VI* in its most acute form. There are of course several other strands of action that seem to dangle somewhat embarrassingly from the play—the Winchester-Gloucester disputes, the issue of Plantagenet's inheritance, the Suffolk-Margaret courtship—but each of them can at least be rationalized as preparatory for events in Part II. Only the Auvergne episode stands entirely self-contained. Although most modern critics are sympathetically aware of the non-Aristotelian bases of Elizabethan dramatic form, their reactions to this scene suggest considerable discomfort with so flagrant a violation of the principle of unity of action. The two most penetrating accounts of the play, for example, rather curiously shy away from the episode. In *Shakespeare's Heroical Histories* (Cambridge, Mass., 1971), David Riggs omits all mention of it, while J. P. Brockbank huddles its effect into a single sentence: "Talbot's stratagem at Auvergne ... is not subtle-witted but represents the triumph of soldierly resourcefulness over French and female craft."[1] M. M. Reese's

---

[1] "The Frame of Disorder: *Henry VI*," in *Early Shakespeare* (Stratford-upon-Avon Studies 3), ed. John Russell Brown and Bernard Harris (New York, 1961), p. 78.

indecisive response suggests a high degree of aesthetic frustration: "Probably the scene is purely symbolic, to proclaim that the true champions of England are proof against fleshly lures; but it may have been written with topical intent, to warn some unknown Elizabethan captain of the dangers of combining war with amorous dalliance."[2] Even so sympathetic an apologist as E. M. W. Tillyard sees the episode as evidence that in his immaturity Shakespeare "occasionally satisfies the taste for the startling but irrelevant anecdote; the pieces of sensation that pleased the people but could be spared from the play."[3]

The problem is complicated by the fact that such scenes are not confined to *1 Henry VI*. Indeed, exact analogues occur in each play of the tetralogy. The "miracle" of Saint Albans in Part II, for example, seems equally obtrusive and, in terms of unity of action, dramatically inconsequential; the same can be said of the "mole-hill" scene in Part III and the wooing of Anne in *Richard III*. With the exception of Richard's wooing sequence, moreover, which occurs in Act I, Scene ii, each of these episodes is placed at roughly the same point in the dramatic action, early or midway in Act II. The existence of such analogues and the obvious artistry of the later ones suggest strongly that more than sensationalism may be at work in *1 Henry VI*.

Once one grows suspicious of a specialized function for such scenes, patterns of relevance gradually emerge. At the most obvious level, the Countess of Auvergne serves as one of a trio of temptresses, all of whom are French, associated with witchcraft, and potential emasculators of their victims; all figure prominently in episodes that perform a set of variations on the theme of love versus war.[4] Charles the Dauphin is overcome by the first of these temptresses, Joan La Pucelle, in a physical combat rich with amatory innuendo. Vanquished by her sword, he becomes her sexual thrall:

> Impatiently I burn with thy desire;
> My heart and hands thou hast at once subdu'd.
> Excellent Pucelle, if thy name be so,
> Let me thy servant and not sovereign be. . . .
>
> [I.ii.108-11][5]

---

[2] *The Cease of Majesty* (New York, 1961), p. 171.

[3] *Shakespeare's History Plays* (London, 1944), p. 183. For a provocative interpretation of the scene that differs radically from mine, see Sigurd Burckhardt, *Shakespearean Meanings* (Princeton, 1968), pp. 47-77.

[4] For a useful account of the play's female roles, see David M. Bevington, "The Domineering Female in *1 Henry VI*," Shakespeare Studies, 2 (1966), 51-58.

[5] All citations to *1 Henry VI* are from the Arden edition of Andrew S. Cairncross (London, 1962).

Joan's conquest signifies not only a shameful reversal of Charles's masculine and kingly roles, but, in the witty equivocation on her title—*pucelle* or *puzzel, maid* or *whore*—an ironic reversal of Petrarchan convention as well. (Shakespeare had discovered long before *Macbeth,* it appears, the equivocation of the fiend.) Framing the scene are allusions to the topos that underlies this inversion of heroic values: Charles enters, bemused by the vagaries of "Mars his true moving," and exits, enamored of his "Bright star of Venus, fall'n down on earth...."

Analogous reversals occur at the end of the play in Suffolk's "capture" of Margaret of Anjou and Henry's subsequent infatuation. As Pucelle is led off to the stake in Act V, Suffolk enters "with Margaret *in his hand.*" "Be what thou wilt," he says, "thou art my prisoner." But at the exchange of a glance the captor becomes captive:

> O fairest beauty, do not fear nor fly!
> For I will touch thee but with reverent hands,
> And lay them gently on thy tender side.
> I kiss these fingers for eternal peace.
>
> [V.iii.45-49]

If it is by a kind of metempsychosis that Margaret becomes inspired with Pucelle's witchcraft at the moment of her death, a similarly mysterious psychic energy inflates Suffolk's rhetoric to the extent that it bewitches the king. It is a heady Petrarchism indeed that can provoke at second hand a response like Henry's:

> I feel such sharp dissension in my breast,
> Such fierce alarums both of hope and fear,
> As I am sick with working of my thoughts.
> Take therefore shipping; post, my lord, to France;
> Agree to any covenants, and procure
> That Lady Margaret do vouchsafe to come
> To cross the seas to England and be crown'd
> King Henry's faithful and anointed queen.
>
> [V.v.84-91]

Having ended one war with an inauspicious contract, Henry now ends another, this one in his breast, in like manner. Ironically, of course, the capitulation to Venus, involving as it does a violation of his betrothal to the daughter of the earl of Armagnac and an abrogation of his duties as king, will bring peace neither to Henry nor to the realm.

The interplay between love and war exerted a peculiar fascination upon Elizabethan writers, as is illustrated in two works that seem especially pertinent to *1 Henry VI.* In Robert Greene's

Euphues His Censure to Philautus (1587), Achilles tells Polixena that "beauty is of more vigour then prowesse, and affection a sorer enemy to resist then fortitude. *Hercules* found the sight of Deianyra more perilous than all the rest of his travells. *Mars* had rather oppose him selfe against all the Gods, then enter a jarre with Venus."[6] Talbot is linked to Hercules on two occasions, in the Auvergne episode (II.iii.18) and in Lucy's celebration of his titles upon his death in battle (IV.vii.60). In the anonymous *Edward III* the convention achieves delightful sophistication as Edward, languishing with love when he should be invading France, vents his illicit passion for the Countess of Salisbury:

> The quarrel, that I have, requires no arms
> But these of mine; and these shall meet my foe
> In a deep march of penetrable groans:
> My eyes shall be my arrows; and my sighs
> Shall serve me as the vantage of the wind,
> To whirl away my sweet'st artillery:
> Ah but, alas, she wins the sun of me,
> For that is she herself; and thence it comes
> That poets term the wanton warrior blind. . . .[7]

The entire episode with the Countess, which affords many parallels with the Auvergne scene in *1 Henry VI*, has been often attributed to Shakespeare.[8]

If Charles, Suffolk, and Henry play Mars to their respective Venuses, Talbot withstands the venerian lures with the heroism of Aeneas—unaided, moreover, by the prodding of Jupiter. Upon his invitation to visit the Countess, his two companions, Burgundy and Bedford, respond with knowing glances and the inevitable military innuendos:

> Nay, then, I see our wars
> Will turn into a peaceful comic sport,
> When ladies crave to be encounter'd with.
>
> [II.ii.44-46]

Talbot, meanwhile, as is shown by his whispered aside to his captain, is making plans. As she awaits her victim, the Countess soliloquizes in terms that make it clear that the encounter will consist of a military venture undreamed of by Burgundy or Bedford:

---

[6] *Life and Complete Works*, ed. Alexander B. Grosart (1881-86; rpt. New York, 1964), VI, 160.

[7] *Elizabethan History Plays*, ed. William A. Armstrong (London, 1965), p. 116.

[8] See Irving Ribner, *The English History Play in the Age of Shakespeare* (New York, 1965), pp. 142-43.

1 Henry VI: Chivalry and Ceremony

> The plot is laid; if all things fall out right,
> I shall as famous be by this exploit,
> As Scythian Tomyris by Cyrus' death.
>
> [II.iii.4-6]

Talbot's resistance to amorous distraction in such circumstances provides a significant measure of his heroism, just as the susceptibility of his compatriots—including, later, his king—demonstrates their easy fallibility. That in doing so he exhibits something of the wit and grace of Gawain in Bercilak's castle provides a measure of Shakespeare's early sophistication and the remarkable continuity of English aristocratic values.

The ideal of chivalric resistance to venerian irrationality threads its way throughout Shakespeare's career, finding perhaps its quintessential expression in the emblem of controlled passion provided in *The Tempest* by the figures of Ferdinand and Miranda seated in Prospero's cave, playing chess (V.i). In the histories, committed as they are to the world of politics and power unrefracted by the artifice of play, the ideal finds a less romantic fulfillment. Much of what often offends a modern audience in Henry V's wooing of Katharine, for example, springs directly from Shakespeare's refusal to romanticize a marriage that is primarily one of political convenience. Henry's courtship constitutes in its own terms a distinct political threat, as dangerous, perhaps, as Agincourt itself. When it is announced that the French king has agreed to all but a single article of the treaty—the provision that Henry be addressed as *Roy d'Angleterre, Heritier de France*—one is inclined to expect an English gesture of magnanimity; instead, Henry firmly takes all:

> I pray you then, in love and dear alliance,
> Let that one article rank with the rest;
> And thereupon give me your daughter.
>
> [V.ii.363-65] [9]

It is not that Henry's affection for Katharine is insincere but that he allows neither the exhilaration of victory nor the heady wine of romance to disorder his sense of priorities. That in the midst of his wooing Henry looks forward to begetting a valiant son, one who "shall go to Constantinople and take the Turk by the beard" (ll. 217-28), suggests that Shakespeare conceived the scene with more than a casual recollection of Henry VI's failure as peacemaker and wooer.

---

[9] All citations to *Henry V* are from the Arden edition of J. H. Walter (London, 1954).

The Countess of Auvergne episode, then, functions at the very least as one of a series of scenes that define in political and military terms the value of chastity (in the Elizabethan sense, of course, of rational control of sexual passion). The full implications of the episode, however, run deeper than this and reach farther toward the conceptual center of the play. In order to perceive them, one must attend to the nuances of the courtly conversation by means of which Talbot not only enchants but educates his temptress. The focal point of their exchange consists of a witty opposition between the notions of substance and shadow: "Long time thy shadow hath been thrall to me," the Countess gloats, "For in my gallery thy picture hangs; / And now the substance shall endure the like . . ." (II.iii.35-37). Talbot's burst of laughter at this point unsettles the Countess and provokes the following dialogue:

Tal.   I laugh to see your ladyship so fond
        To think that you have aught but Talbot's shadow
        Whereon to practise your severity.
Count. Why, art not thou the man?
Tal.   I am indeed.
Count. Then have I substance too.
Tal.   No, no, I am but shadow of myself:
        You are deceiv'd, my substance is not here;
        For what you see is but the smallest part
        And least proportion of humanity;
        I tell you madam, were the whole frame here,
        It is of such a spacious lofty pitch
        Your roof were not sufficient to contain't.
                                          [II.iii.44-55]

The riddle is unriddled, of course, by the entry of Talbot's soldiers:

        How say you, madam? Are you now persuaded
        That Talbot is but shadow of himself?
        These are his substance, sinews, arms, and strength,
        With which he yoketh your rebellious necks,
        Razeth your cities, and subverts your towns,
        And in a moment makes them desolate.
                                          [II.iii.60-65]

The point of Talbot's conundrum seems clear enough: without his troops a commander is powerless, a mere shadow. Talbot's application of this truism enables him to defeat the Countess, since a lesser man, a vaunter, would have accepted her invitation as

1 Henry VI: Chivalry and Ceremony

recognition of his *own* worth and been captured alone. The Countess's invitation, expressing as it did her desire "That she may boast she hath beheld the man / Whose glory fills the world with loud report" (II.ii.42-43), encouraged such a vaunting response, and added, therefore, to the bait of amorous intrigue the even more insidious lure of pride.

If the matter of Talbot's riddle thus contributes an added dimension to the nature of his victory, its manner of expression further complicates and extends its significance. The division between substance and shadow, for example, is potentially misleading. It is not that Talbot is merely shadow, his troops substance, but that one is incomplete without the other; when acting in consort, the two form a single entity. Only with this meaning in mind can one feel the full weight of Talbot's equivocation, "I am but shadow of *myself.*" What the Countess sees before her—"the smallest part / And least proportion of humanity"—is merely one side of Talbot's being, his "self" divided from his troops; it is also (the phrase is ambiguous) merely Talbot's body, his physical as opposed to his spiritual self. Hence the Countess's earlier scornful astonishment at Talbot's unimpressive physique:

> Is this the Scourge of France?
> Is this the Talbot, so much fear'd abroad
> That with his name the mothers still their babes?
> I see report is fabulous and false:
> I thought I should have seen some Hercules,
> A second Hector, for his grim aspect
> And large proportion of his strong-knit limbs.
> Alas, this is a child, a silly dwarf!
> It cannot be this weak and writhled shrimp
> Should strike such terror to his enemies.
>
> [II.iii.14-23]

The Countess fails to trap Talbot because she conceives of heroism in conventional terms; for her it implies vaunting self-assertion and tremendous physical strength. Talbot escapes her trap because he recognizes the insignificance of bodily force and the vulnerability of a man alone. When Talbot's "frame" arrives, it supports his "shadow"—recall the portrait in the Countess's gallery—and makes it part of a unified whole.[10] The scene draws to its conclusion with a terse and witty expression of the Countess's new insight:

---

[10]Although the Arden editor follows John Dover Wilson's gloss on *frame*—"apt at once to a building and to the human body"—the context suggests as well an allusion to picture frames; the dichotomy between substance and shadow grows naturally out of the

> Victorious Talbot, pardon my abuse;
> I find thou art no less than fame hath bruited,
> And more than may be gather'd by thy shape.
>
> [II.iii.66-68]

The Auvergne episode thus articulates through Talbot an ideal that includes, but goes beyond, chastity—an ideal of chivalric community. The Countess's final attitude toward Talbot derives from her new perception that true heroism lies not in individualistic self-assertion but in loyalty to a whole that transcends the self and gives it meaning. It is this ideal of community, manifested in Talbot's every action, that animates and unifies the play. Its most compressed and emblematic expression occurs when at Paris Talbot pays homage to the king:

> My gracious Prince, and honourable peers,
> Hearing of your arrival in this realm,
> I have awhile given truce unto my wars
> To do my duty to my sovereign:
> In sign whereof, this arm, that hath reclaim'd
> To your obedience fifty fortresses,
> Twelve cities, and seven walled towns of strength,
> Beside five hundred prisoners of esteem,
> Lets fall his sword before your Highness' feet;
> And with submissive loyalty of heart
> Ascribes the glory of his conquest got
> First to my God, and next unto your Grace. [*Kneels*]
>
> [III.iv.1-12]

That the ideal is a traditional one in no way vitiates its emotional resonance, extended in this instance by the subtle pressures of syntactical movement. As the period sweeps from the initial stress

---

Countess's observation that Talbot's portrait hangs in her gallery. The word *shadow* was often "applied rhetorically to a portrait as contrasted with the original," according to the *Oxford English Dictionary*; *Two Gentlemen of Verona* provides an example:

"*Proteus*. Madam, if your heart be so obdurate,
Vouchsafe me yet your picture for my love,
The picture that is hanging in your chamber;
To that I'll speak, to that I'll sigh and weep;
For, since the substance of your perfect self
Is else devoted, I am but a shadow;
And to your shadow will I make true love" (IV.ii.115-21).

Shakespeare's Sonnet 24 contains the earliest instance cited by the *OED* of the word *frame* referring to a device for supporting pictures:

"Mine eye hath play'd the painter and hath stell'd
Thy beauty's form in table of my heart;
My body is the frame wherein 'tis held . . ."

on Talbot's arm, with its hyperbolic conquests and hints of vaunting self-assertion, to the action of that arm, as it lets fall the sword and (as the synecdoche becomes explicit) ascribes its glory to God and king, one is compelled to experience with Talbot the very redefinition of self that constitutes the heroic ideal.

I have concentrated thus far on the Auvergne episode, not only because its intrinsic merits and thematic significance have often gone unnoticed, but because it carries to an extreme formal tendencies characteristic of the tetralogy as a whole. As recent scholarship has made clear, moreover, these tendencies are not unique to the *Henry VI* series but occur generally in plays of the 1580s and early 1590s and in the moralities that preceded them. The context that G. K. Hunter establishes for his illuminating study of the theme of justice in *The Spanish Tragedy* is relevant as well to *1 Henry VI*:

> The assumption that the Elizabethan play inherited from the Tudor interlude a diffuse form which reflects mere incompetence—this becomes increasingly difficult to sustain in the light of recent studies of the interlude by Craik, Spivack, Bevington, and Habicht. These, in their different ways, present the interlude as a serious form, in which flat characterization, repetitiveness, and dependence on a multiplicity of short episodes are not defects, but rather means perfectly adapted to express that age's moral and religious (rather than psychological or social) view of human destiny. Persons are seen to be less important than theme; they exist to illustrate rather than represent; and narrative line gives way to the illustration of doctrine.[11]

Hence those features of the Countess of Auvergne episode that distress critics influenced by neoclassical or naturalistic attitudes toward drama can be seen as extensions and elaborations of a distinctively Elizabethan mode. As Shakespeare's art develops, his use of this mode grows increasingly complex: personality and theme become subtly interdependent, didacticism yields to dialectic, and "doctrine" is no longer "illustrated" but explored in action.

The consequences of this emblematic mode are especially apparent in characterization. In *1 Henry VI*, for example, and

---

[11]"Ironies of Justice in *The Spanish Tragedy*," *Renaissance Drama*, 8 (1965), 91. Hunter's references are to T. W. Craik, *The Tudor Interlude* (Leicester, 1958); Bernard Spivack, *Shakespeare and the Allegory of Evil* (New York, 1958); David M. Bevington, *From Mankind to Marlowe*; and Werner Habicht, "Sénèque et le théâtre pre-Shakespearian," in *Sénèque et le théâtre de la Renaissance*, ed. Jean Jacquot (Paris, 1964). See also Jocelyn Powell, "Marlowe's Spectacle," *Tulane Drama Review*, 8 (1963-64), 195-210.

throughout the tetralogy, personality is invariably subordinated to what can be broadly called theme. In the mature plays this is not the case—both elements being indissolubly joined and mutually supportive. Prince Hal serves at once as the thematic center of *1 Henry IV* and a fully realized individual; Talbot, though fleshed out at isolated moments—in his graceful wit before the Countess, for example—functions mainly as a personification of the chivalric ideal. Although not quiet personifications—and here the method diverges from the morality tradition—the other characters in *1 Henry VI* suffer similar limitations; they too are defined primarily in relation to the ideal that Talbot embodies. In regarding these characters, one is drawn to look through traits of "personality" toward their essential significance, as if they were figures of glass, magnifying, refracting, or distorting the central values of the play.

Even Joan of Arc, whose colloquial vigor and irreverence prove so endearing to modern sensibilities, functions primarily as an antitype to Talbot, a parody of all that he represents.[12] Joan's so-called patriotism, which has been as seductive to some critics as it is to the turncoat Burgundy, is a grotesque inversion of Talbot's—true patriotism involving not merely a passionate love of country but a whole network of loyalties extending from the individual to the deity.[13] Talbot's "self," as we have seen, stretches outward to include his troops, his king, his God. Not so, however, with Joan's. Talbot's love for his son is counterbalanced by Joan's repudiation of her father; his loyalty to his peers, Salisbury and Bedford, by her last-ditch paternity suit against Charles, Alençon, and Reignier; his reverence to his king by her domination of Charles; his piety by her pact with the devil. One doubts whether even the authors of the official homilies would have approved the degree of national allegiance Joan avows in her final plea to her reluctant fiends:

> Cannot my body nor blood-sacrifice
> Entreat you to your wonted furtherance?
> Then take my soul; my body, soul, and all,
> Before that England give the French the foil.
>
> [V.iii.20-23]

Her attempt to save her own life after her capture at the cost of national disgrace is the reductio ad absurdum of an individualism that will ironically eventuate in the destruction of England itself.

---

[12] For an excellent discussion of Joan's parodic role, see David Riggs, *Shakespeare's Heroical Histories* (Cambridge, Mass., 1971), pp. 104-7; the entire chapter on *1 Henry VI* is illuminating.

[13] In "The Frame of Disorder: *Henry VI*," for example, Brockbank cites Joan's wooing of Burgundy as evidence of "an authentic French patriotism" (p. 80).

1 Henry VI: Chivalry and Ceremony

By far the most influential interpretation of Joan's role in *1 Henry VI* has been that of E. M. W. Tillyard, an interpretation which has such important implications for the tetralogy as a whole that it must be examined with some care. As is generally known, Tillyard finds in Shakespeare's histories a theory of providential design that purportedly originates in *Hall's Chronicle*. For Tillyard the premature death of Henry V, the diabolic actions of La Pucelle, and the defeat of Talbot all spring from the same source: God's vengeance for the deposition and murder of his "deputy on earth," Richard II.[14] The single most important obstacle to this so-called Tudor myth lies in the fact that *1 Henry VI* contains no reference to such a curse. Richard II is mentioned only once, in the scene that informs the audience of the nature of Plantagenet's title to the throne (II.v). The discussion between Plantagenet and Mortimer, however, is singularly free of providential overtones and focuses instead, with characteristic Yorkist straightforwardness, on political realities. It is without a glimmer of concern for the memory of Richard II that Plantagenet hastens at the end of the scene to Parliament, "Either to be restored to my blood, / Or make mine ill th'advantage of my good" (II.v.128-29). In order to defend Tillyard's view, one must appeal to the underlying attitudes of an Elizabethan audience, a risky procedure at best, but in this instance impossible. What Tillyard calls the "Tudor myth" is demonstrably not central to Elizabethan conceptions of history. In narrating the reign of Henry VI, neither Hall nor Holinshed alludes to the possibility of divine retribution for the deposition and murder of Richard II. A reading of the chronicles, in fact, once one gets beyond Hall's Preface and Table of Contents, yields massive contradiction, inconsistency, and confusion on the workings of God's will throughout the period covered by both tetralogies. The conclusion of Henry A. Kelly's meticulous examination of the historical sources is authoritative: "the providential aspect of the Tudor myth as described by Mr. Tillyard is an ex post facto Platonic Form, made up of many fragments that were never fitted together into a mental pattern until they felt the force of his own synthesizing energy."[15]

The peculiar influence of Tillyard's view derives in part, one suspects, from its apparent appropriateness to the conclusion of *Richard II*. There are important objections, however, to this line

---

[14]Tillyard, p. 190. Tillyard's view is accepted, with a few qualifications and modifications, by M.M. Reese in *The Cease of Majesty* (pp. 166-67) and Irving Ribner in *The English History Play in the Age of Shakespeare* (New York, 1965), pp. 96, 105.

[15]*Divine Providence in the England of Shakespeare's Histories* (Cambridge, Mass., 1970), p. 298.

of thought. To infer from a later play attributes in an early one is in itself a questionable procedure. The vision of Providence in the later play, moreover, offers little to support Tillyard's claim. Carlisle's famous prophecy in the deposition scene, that "future ages [shall] groan for this foul act" (IV.i.138), though resonant with providential overtones, is only one of several intimations of the world to come.[16] Richard's prophecy that Northumberland and Bolingbroke will soon be at odds because "the love of wicked men converts to fear" (V.i.66) conveys moral and psychological, rather than overtly providential, implications. And Bolingbroke's own anxieties look forward to a future wondrously ironic:

> Can no man tell me of my unthrifty son?
> 'Tis full three months since I did see him last.
> If any plague hang over us, 'tis he.
>
> [V.iii.1-3]

Although this perspective on future events does not quite cancel out the awesome force of Carlisle's images of divine retribution, the complexities it introduces cannot help but provoke in the audience a feeling that the God who will plague England with Henry V works indeed in mysterious ways. The multiple ironies of such a providential design seem unlikely supports for a conception of divine vengeance as simplistic as that which supposedly operates in *1 Henry VI.*

In spite of its defects, Tillyard's interpretation of Joan achieves a certain plausibility because he focuses more on her demonic powers than on the origin or nature of the curse she purportedly fulfills. That Joan is a witch who once calls herself "the English scourge" (I.ii.129) is a fact that leads naturally enough to Tillyard's central questions: "Who but God has assigned her this duty? ... What were the sins God sought to punish?"[17] As A. L. French has amply demonstrated, however, Tillyard's evidence for Joan's role as scourge is scanty at best, depending as it does on a few vague allusions and ambiguous contexts; indeed, Talbot himself is called the "French scourge," not once but three times.[18] In the face of questionable evidence, the questions themselves come to seem suspiciously naive. Witches, after all, fulfilled a variety of functions in the Elizabethan scheme of things, sometimes serving as God's agents, more often Satan's; sometimes

---

[16] All citations to *Richard II* are from the Arden edition of Peter Ure (London, 1961).
[17] Tillyard, p. 190.
[18] "Joan of Arc and *Henry VI*," *English Studies*, 49 (1969), 425-29; for Talbot as scourge see II.iii.14, IV.ii.16, IV.vii.77.

1 Henry VI: Chivalry and Ceremony

punishing sins, more often diabolically inciting them.[19] From a perspective as remote as heaven, of course, one can say that all witchcraft is providential, but from such a vantage point the concept itself ceases to be meaningful.

To deny that *1 Henry VI* depicts God's punishment of England through foreign witchcraft is not to deny the existence of metaphysical implications in Joan's role. Indeed, one of the chief reasons for pursuing Tillyard's argument at such length is that it calls attention to one of the most problematic aspects of the play. The metaphysical is most obtrusive in the mysterious appearance of Joan's fiends and their subsequent refusal of aid, but its presence is felt as well in her "enchantment" of Burgundy and in her unnatural military prowess and success. No sooner has La Pucelle lent her mystique to the French than the Master Gunner's boy, heretofore utterly ineffective as a marksman, kills Gargrave and Salisbury as they stand on the turrets overlooking Orleans. Talbot himself invests this deed with metaphysical significance:

> What chance is this that suddenly hath cross'd us?
> . . . . .
> Accursed tower! Accursed fatal hand
> That hath contriv'd this woeful tragedy!
>
> [I.iv. 71-76]

Talbot's astonishing inability to defeat Joan in their only encounter suggests more poignantly the mysterious nature of the power she possesses:

> My thoughts are whirled like a potter's wheel;
> I know not what I am, nor what I do:
> A witch by fear, not force, like Hannibal,
> Drives back our troops and conquers as she lists. . . .
>
> [I.v.19-22]

The problem that Joan's witchcraft poses, if one rejects Tillyard's thesis, is that it seems to originate in no special curse and, even more curiously, to issue in no concrete results. That Joan's encounter with Talbot ends in a standoff is emblematic of the nature of the war as a whole; despite her diabolic leadership, the French forces never gain more than a temporary victory until the end of the play, at which point they acquire through Henry's negligence rather than their own might an ignominious peace. At the very moment when Joan's powers should be most dramatically

---

[19] For a thorough review of the practices and beliefs governing Elizabethan witchcraft, see Keith Thomas, *Religion and the Decline of Magic* (London, 1971), pp. 435-583, esp. pp. 469-77, 493-501.

displayed—at Talbot's death, after which her fiends abandon her—Shakespeare explicitly reduces them to insignificance in the words of Lucy:

> The fraud of England, not the force of France,
> Hath now entrapp'd the noble-minded Talbot:
> Never to England shall he bear his life,
> But die betray'd to fortune by your strife.
>
> [IV.iv.36-39]

The play's overt didacticism, though crude enough, at least insures attention to its points of emphasis. Lucy's accusation of York and Somerset is one of five unequivocal assertions, usually in soliloquy, which assign sole responsibility for England's plight to civil dissension.[20] Exeter's ominous pronouncement after the disruption of Henry's coronation is typically precise:

> no simple man that sees
> This jarring discord of nobility,
> This shouldering of each other in the Court,
> This factious bandying of their favorites,
> But sees it doth presage some ill event.
> 'Tis much when sceptres are in children's hands;
> But more when envy breeds unkind division:
> There comes the ruin, there begins confusion.
>
> [IV.i.187-94]

The stridency of the tone as well as the reiterations of the theme suggest that the message is obliquely topical.

The play's structure, moreover, implicitly reenforces this didactic current. Scene one, for example, embodies in miniature a causal chain that later determines the movement of the play as a whole. When Exeter responds to the announced loss of French territories with the questions, "How were they lost? What treachery was us'd?" the First Messenger replies:

> No treachery, but want of men and money.
> Amongst the soldiers this is muttered—
> That here you maintain several factions:
> And whilst a field should be dispatch'd and fought,
> You are disputing of your generals. . . .
>
> [I.i.69-73]

A special credence is lent to the messenger's analysis by the fact that the wrangling of Winchester and Gloucester immediately precedes his entrance. The announcements that follow, moreover, depict conditions that seem the natural consequences of such

---

[20] See III.i.65-73, 187-201; IV.i.182-94; IV.iii.47-53.

dissension: the growth in French unity, symbolized by the Dauphin's coronation; the retreat of Talbot, which places him in such straits that the cowardly Falstaff collapses under pressure and flees. In the larger movement of the play, disorder at home spreads in a similar manner throughout all the great centers of national unity—Westminster Abbey, the Tower, the Temple Garden, Parliament—and then, as the court goes abroad, to Paris and the battlefield at Bordeaux, where Talbot's death, the ultimate consequence of civil dissension, marks the end of the communal ideal.

Given such an overwhelming emphasis on moral causation, it becomes difficult to account for the play's consistent though unrealized gestures toward the metaphysical. If one considers the direction of Shakespeare's later development, however, these gestures take on a new significance. It is a commonplace that one of the distinctive features of mature Shakespearean tragedy is its mysterious and often paradoxical fusion of moral and metaphysical causation. The paradigmatic Shakespearean tragedy, say *Macbeth*, springs from a conjunction of character, social pressure, and, by whatever name, fate. If one is philosophically inclined, one's estimate of the tragedies is likely to depend on the relative profundity of these causes and the subtlety of their interpenetration. As is typical of the early tragedies, *Romeo and Juliet* significantly de-emphasizes one of these elements—that of character. Though the two lovers are in some sense victims of their own passions, the twin themes of fate and feuding—conjoined in the Prologue's allusion to the "fatal loins of these two foes" from which the "star-crossed lovers take their life"—dominate the action. In *1 Henry VI,* centering as it does on the experience of the nation rather than an individual, the question of character becomes irrelevant or, more precisely, is generalized to include the whole of society. That Shakespeare hints at the presence of underlying metaphysical causes suggests, I believe, a reaching out toward the philosophical poise of the mature tragedies and histories; that he ultimately sacrifices this dimension of experience for the more narrowly political and ethical reveals the strength of his didactic urge—a strength manifested repeatedly in the homilies of Exeter and Lucy.

The death of Talbot, then, is generated not by any providential design external to the world of the play but by the social pressures building up within it. The death scene itself serves as the play's climactic moment of social disintegration, the moment when Talbot calls for troops that do not appear. Prefaced as it is by the shameful betrayals of York and Somerset, the scene achieves its effects within an ironic framework of national disgrace. Its ultimate impact, however, is emotionally quite complex, as is partly suggested by the vivid contemporary appreciation of Thomas Nashe: "How would it have joyed brave *Talbot* (the terror of the French) to thinke that after he had lyne two hundred years in his Tombe, hee should triumphe againe on the Stage, and have his bones newe embalmed with the teares of ten thousand spectators at least (at severall times), who, in the Tragedian that represents his person, imagine they behold him fresh bleeding."[21] In celebrating with the rich metaphor of embalming tears the audience's sense of communion with its heroic past, Nashe emphasizes qualities in the scene that contribute considerably to its emotional depth. Talbot's death is indeed heroic and is expressed with a stylistic elaboration that strives to match its greatness:

> Thou antic Death, which laugh'st us here to scorn,
> Anon, from thy insulting tyranny,
> Coupled in bonds of perpetuity,
> Two Talbots winged through the lither sky,
> In thy despite shall scape mortality.
>
> [IV.vii.18-22][22]

Unlike Joan of Arc, whose eternal rewards consist of the fires of hell and everlasting infamy, Talbot and his son gain heaven and the tears of ten thousand spectators. That the "bonds of perpetuity" merely link together two Talbots, however, brings to mind once more the ironic underpinnings Nashe chooses to ignore: the community that once sustained Talbot has now shrunk to that between father and son, and with their death will be no more. Talbot's dying words leave one with a final image of the strength and smallness of those bonds: "Soldiers, adieu! I have what I would have, / Now my old arms are young John Talbot's grave" (IV.vii. 31-32). Thus expires the chivalric ideal.

Complex ironies created by the juxtaposition of scenes or of contrasting perspectives become, of course, a distinguishing feature of mature Shakespearean drama. The temptation among critics examining the early plays is to discover retrospectively a higher degree of complexity than actually exists, as would be the

---

[21] *The Works of Thomas Nashe*, ed. Ronald B. McKerrow, I (London, 1904), 212. Here and throughout I have normalized *u, v, i, j*, the long *s*, superscript letters, and contractions.

[22] Samuel Johnson, mystified by the use of rhyme, speculates that the lines were part of a previously written poem "copied here only to save the trouble of composing new." See *Johnson on Shakespeare*, ed. Arthur Sherbo, Yale Edition of the Works of Samuel Johnson, VIII (New Haven, 1968), 575-77.

case, for example, if one saw in Talbot's unawareness of the machinations that doom him a critique of his sufficiency as a heroic ideal. An even more seductive example lurks in the clash between Joan and Lucy, which brings the death scene to its close:

Lucy. But where's the great Alcides of the field,
Valiant Lord Talbot, Earl of Shrewsbury,
Created for his rare success in arms
Great Earl of Washford, Waterford, and Valence,
Lord Talbot of Goodrig and Urchinfield,
Lord Strange of Blackmere, Lord Verdun of Alton,
Cromwell of Wingfield, Furnival of Sheffield,
The thrice victorious Lord of Falconbridge,
Knight of the noble Order of Saint George,
Worthy Saint Michael, and the Golden Fleece,
Great Marshal to Henry the Sixth
Of all his wars within the realm of France?
Puc. Here is a silly-stately style indeed!
The Turk, that two and fifty kingdoms hath,
Writes not so tedious a style as this.
Him that thou magnifiest with all these titles,
Stinking and fly-blown lies here at our feet.

[IV.vii.60-76]

For the modern reader Joan's irreverent vitality (determined, ironically, more by her parodic role than force of "personality") seems infinitely more appealing than Lucy's rhetoric or even Talbot's virtue. In many ways Joan foreshadows Falstaff, anticipating in her sarcasm, her indifference to honor in the face of physical reality, her witty perception of life's incongruities, the fat knight's response to the corpse of Sir Walter Blount on the field at Shrewsbury: "There's honor for you! Here's no vanity" (*1 Henry IV* V.iii.33).[23]

It is as important not to read retroactive ironies into the encounter between Joan and Lucy, however, as it is to remain open to the full range of Falstaff's appeal. Consider, for example, Leslie A. Fiedler's reaction to their exchange:

After this grandiloquence [Lucy's], the Pucelle answers so quietly and with such good sense that for one instant the balance of Shakespeare's sympathy (along with ours) tilts in her direction. For the first time in his career, perhaps, he betrays his ambivalence about the reigning values of his time, his suspicion, later expressed in certain speeches of Shylock and Caliban, that by virtue of his strangeness the stranger in our midst can sometimes see the

---

[23]All citations to *1 Henry IV* are from the Arden edition of A. R. Humphreys (London, 1960).

silliness of the games we play in deadly earnest. And though such perceptions are not all the truth they are, like Joan's rejoinder, *also* true.[24]

Such a response, it seems to me, reflects above all an insensitivity to the dramatic mode at work. If the conventions governing the scene were those of dramatic realism, then Lucy would be guilty of grandiloquence or worse. But his language is in fact as decorous as the couplets with which Talbot meets his death. Neither Lucy's nor Joan's rhetoric is dramatically realistic in intent or effect. Lucy's celebration of Talbot, in fact, paraphrases the inscription on his tomb at Rouen,[25] while the terms of Joan's debunking depend upon a most improbable acceleration in the normal processes of decay. That La Pucelle cannot comprehend Lucy's style merely demonstrates her ignorance of the spiritual realities to which it bears witness. What lies at Joan's feet, as we know from the Countess of Auvergne episode, is "but the smallest part / And least proportion of humanity"—that part which Joan, in her final moments, tries deceitfully and fruitlessly to save. While Joan observes his body, Talbot's spirit wings its way to immortality. Given the values consistently embodied in Talbot's life, values that achieve their apotheosis in the lyricism of his death, there is no way in which Joan's rejoinder could be "*also* true."

The resemblance between Joan's encounter with Lucy and Falstaff's with Blount's corpse points to one of the essential continuities in Shakespeare's development as a dramatist. In the later plays, however, the moral and psychological pressures generated by such juxtapositions become considerably more explosive. The act of discriminating between Joan and Talbot, or Lucy, does not engage one's deepest intellectual or emotional capacities: the polarities consist of moral absolutes, allegorically opposed. In *1 Henry IV,* on the other hand, the subtlety and range of moral definition stretches these capacities to the utmost, sometimes, it seems, to the breaking point. The polarities still exist in *1 Henry IV,* of course, but they have been vastly enriched and redefined in such a way as to make the hero, unlike Talbot, their middle term. Standing between two misdirected extremes, the idealism of Hotspur and the realism of Falstaff, Prince Hal embodies an ideal both more precisely articulated than Talbot's and more finely attuned to the complexities of human experience.

[24]*The Stranger in Shakespeare* (New York, 1972), p. 57. Fiedler is also curiously insensitive to the (admittedly premodern) mythic grandeur of Talbot: "Talbot is a provincial hero and Joan a universal myth, a figure of inexhaustible archetypal resonance" (p. 58).

[25]See J. Pearce, "An Earlier Talbot Epitaph," *Modern Language Notes,* 59 (1944), 327-29.

1 Henry VI: Chivalry and Ceremony

Hotspur and Falstaff, though not "all the truth," are "*also* true" in ways that La Pucelle is not. In part this added complexity springs from an increased realism of characterization; no one doubts that the opposing personalities of Hotspur and Falstaff create more richly the illusion of life than those of Talbot and Joan. The continuity of technique from *1 Henry VI* to *1 Henry IV,* however, suggests that the psychological density of the mature plays represents not so much a shift in artistic direction as a natural outgrowth of earlier conventions. An observation offered by Martin Price in another context seems pertinent to this aspect of Shakespeare's development: "the elaborate forms of realism are generated less by the desire to represent the actual than by the pressure of conventions reaching outward for more complex differentiation."[26]

That La Pucelle dismisses with contempt Lucy's "stately style" reflects the centrality of symbolism in the play's conception of chivalry. Talbot is not only memorialized in death with an incantation of his titles; he serves throughout the play as a spokesman for a sacramental vision of experience. After the battle of Orleans Talbot leads Salisbury's funeral procession and directs that a monument be raised,

> Upon the which, that every one may read,
> Shall be engrav'd the sack of Orleans,
> The treacherous manner of his mournful death,
> And what a terror he had been to France.
>
> [II.ii.14-17]

After Rouen he likewise eulogizes the duke of Bedford. In Paris Talbot himself is created earl of Shrewsbury in solemn ceremony before the king, and soon thereafter, in a gesture akin to Richard II's "rite of 'degradation,'" he strips the coward Falstaff of his Order of the Garter.[27] Even Talbot's battle cry before Orleans voices this compulsion to wed inner worth with outward form:

> Hark, countrymen! either renew the fight,
> Or tear the lions out of England's coat;
> Renounce your style, give sheep in lions' stead. . . .
>
> [I.v.27-29]

The dichotomy between Talbot's ritualism and La Pucelle's "naturalism" reemerges in *1 Henry IV* when Prince Hal extends to the dead Hotspur "fair rites of tenderness" and Falstaff stabs him

---

[26] "The Irrelevant Detail and the Emergence of Form," in *Aspects of Narrative,* ed. J. Hillis Miller (New York, 1971), p. 74.

[27] For Richard's inversion of the coronation ceremony, see *Richard II,* IV.i.203-21; the phrase is Walter Pater's, in *Appreciations* (London, 1889), pp. 205-6.

in the thigh (V.iv). That La Pucelle's "naturalism" is demonic in origin is a fact not entirely irrelevant to Falstaff, "that old white-bearded Satan" (II.iv.509).

Throughout *1 Henry VI* Joan and her compatriots unconsciously parody Talbot's conception of the significance of ceremony. Joan's interview with her fiends, to whom she attributes all her powers, travesties Talbot's earlier obeisance to King Henry, her "charming spells and periapts" and "ancient incantations" countering the simple dignity of his kneeling. Subtler and wittier are Charles's incessant celebrations of Joan. Compare the French king's fantasy after winning Orleans, for example, with Talbot's commemorations of Bedford and Salisbury:

> 'Tis Joan, not we, by whom the day is won;
> For which I will divide my crown with her,
> And all the priests and friars in my realm
> Shall in procession sing her endless praise.
> A statelier pyramis to her I'll rear
> Than Rhodope's of Memphis ever was;
> In memory of her, when she is dead,
> Her ashes, in an urn more precious
> Than the rich jewel-coffer of Darius,
> Transported shall be at high festivals
> Before the kings and queens of France.
> No longer on Saint Denis will we cry,
> But Joan de Pucelle shall be France's saint.
>
> [I.vi.17-29]

The reference to Rhodopis, a Greek courtesan who married a king of Memphis, provokes a pungent gloss from Samuel Johnson: "I think he means to call her strumpet all the while he is making this loud praise of her."[28] The allusion illuminates Charles's vow to divide his crown; in view of the play's pervasive sexual innuendos, it casts a suspicious glow as well on his desire to raise a pyramid. From both a religious and an aesthetic perspective, the whole exotic mélange of popery and paganism is comically abhorrent. What would one expect of a realm still enamored of the whore of Babylon, after all, but pagan superstition and sainthood for a pucelle?

Talbot's ritualism is a natural extension of the values he represents, the means by which one weds oneself to a community and a tradition. Throughout the play his ceremonial actions symbolize the essential truths imparted in the Countess of Auvergne episode and, more directly, in the choric laments of Exeter and Lucy. It is through the theme of ceremony, moreover,

[28] *Johnson on Shakespeare*, VIII, 569-70.

1 Henry VI: Chivalry and Ceremony

that Talbot's role becomes most completely assimilated into the conception of an ideal society that underlies the play and the tetralogy as a whole. As both theme and mode of dramatic action, ceremony serves at the deepest level to unify the play.

Though central to Elizabethan life and literature, the idea of ceremony, like many deeply rooted cultural presuppositions, scarcely ever received explicit justification. A rare exception occurs in Chapman's continuation of "Hero and Leander," in a passage so immediately relevant to *1 Henry VI* that it is worth quoting at length. The goddess Ceremony, disturbed that the clandestine lovers have taken "substance without rites," appears in a vision to Leander:

> But as he shook with passionate desire
> To put in flame his other secret fire,
> A music so divine did pierce his ear,
> As never yet his ravish'd sense did hear:
> When suddenly a light of twenty hues
> Brake through the roof, and like the rainbow views
> Amaz'd Leander; in whose beams came down
> The goddess Ceremony, with a crown
> Of all the stars, and heaven with her descended;
> Her flaming hair to her bright feet extended,
> By which hung all the bench of deities,
> And in a chain, compact of ears and eyes,
> She led Religion. All her body was
> Clear and transparent as the purest glass:
> For she was all presented to the sense;
> Devotion, Order, State, and Reverence
> Her shadows were; Society, Memory;
> All which her sight made live, her absence die.
>
> . . . . .
>
> One hand a mathematic crystal sways,
> Which gathering in one line a thousand rays
> From her bright eyes, Confusion burns to death,
> And all estates of men distinguisheth.
> By it Morality and Comeliness
> Themselves in all their sightly figures dress.
> Her other hand a laurel rod applies,
> To beat back Barbarism and Avarice,
> That follow'd, eating earth and excrement
> And human limbs, and would make proud ascent
> To seats of gods, were Ceremony slain.
> The Hours and Graces bore her glorious train,
> And all the sweets of our society
> Were spher'd and treasur'd in her bounteous eye.
>
> [III.105-22, 131-44] [29]

[29] Christopher Marlowe, *The Poems,* ed. Millar Maclure (London, 1968).

The process by means of which Chapman created this magnificent abstraction and the extent to which it synthesizes Elizabethan thought on the subject have been admirably explicated by D. J. Gordon.[30] For our own purposes the more recondite allusions can be sacrificed to the central idea: that ceremony is divine in origin, the animating spirit behind all order in religion and the state, the protectress of civilization—in a word, the earthly embodiment of cosmic harmony. Though original in its combination of details, Chapman's personification embodies assumptions about the nature of the universe that, centering as they do on the principle of hierarchical order, are too familiar to need explanation.

When one turns from Chapman's goddess to the opening scene of *1 Henry VI,* one can feel the full impact of its careful design. The ominous roll of the death march, the solemn processional of the funeral cortege, the mournful exaltations of the dead monarch, "Henry the Fifth, too famous to live long"—all conspire to arouse in the audience that tragic yet paradoxically comforting awe by means of which a ritualization of death unifies and sustains the living. The "performance of such ritual acts," as D. J. Gordon remarks with reference to "Hero and Leander," "is acknowledgment of the divine principle of order and enactment of the workings of it; and to enact the workings of the principle brings it into operation."[31] It is in this sense that Chapman can claim for his goddess,

> Devotion, Order, State, and Reverence
> Her shadows were; Society, Memory,
> All which her sight made live, her absence die.

In *1 Henry VI,* however, the opening ritual is at once disrupted, first by the bickering of Winchester and Gloucester, then by the entrance of three messengers in succession, all of whom bring news of English defeats in France. "Guienne, Champaigne, Rheims, Rouen, Orleans, / Paris, Guysors, Poictiers," the inverted litany drones on, "are all quite lost" (I.i.60-61). As the nobles disband in turmoil, the Bishop of Winchester remains on stage to divulge his plans to steal the king and rule the realm. The funeral ceremony has been aborted, Henry V forgotten; the goddess absents herself, her shadows die.

Hence begins what Hereward T. Price calls the "motif of the interrupted ceremony."[32] The play's exploitation of ceremony,

---

[30]"Chapman's *Hero and Leander,*" *English Miscellany,* 5 (1954), 55 ff.
[31]Gordon, p. 61.
[32]"Construction in Shakespeare," *University of Michigan Contributions in Modern Philology,* No. 17 (May 1951), p. 28.

1 Henry VI: Chivalry and Ceremony

indeed, is even more varied and wide-ranging than Price's pioneering structural analysis implies. We have already noticed in the case of the French, for example, what might be described as inverted, rather than interrupted, ceremonies, and in the case of Talbot a ceremonial, or heraldic, use of language. We have observed as well that Talbot, representing as he does the chilvalric ideal of community, embodies the very principles of ceremony, fusing thereby theme and character—broken ceremonies eventually breaking the man. It is not merely the interruption of ceremony upon which the play is structured, then, but the idea of ceremony itself, played out in a remarkable variety of permutations (we shall observe later the paradox of an invented ceremony). Whether in true solemnity or travesty, in emblematic action or character, ceremony pervades the play, providing a constant measure of social disintegration. As a symbol of cosmic harmony, moreover, ceremony imparts to the play more profound metaphysical resonances than any to be felt in Joan's witchcraft or obscure allusions to divine retribution.

As the action of the play alternates between indecisive battles in France and social disorder at home, each communal gathering becomes increasingly divisive. In Act III a meeting in Parliament affords the occasion for the second major instance of disrupted ritual. The scene opens with an emblematic action: "*Flourish. Enter* King, Exeter, Gloucester, Winchester, Warwick, Somerset, Suffolk, Richard Plantagenet. Gloucester *offers to put up a bill*; Winchester *snatches it, tears it*" (III.i.s.d.). Though it will be necessary in discussing *2 Henry VI* to make a distinction between the concepts of ceremony and law, it is obvious that they overlap considerably. Chapman, in fact, as D. J. Gordon points out, gives to his goddess the additional name of Thesme, an adaptation of the Greek word for law.[33] The interdependence of secular and religious authority in Elizabethan England made such a conjunction almost inevitable. In its concern with law, the Parliament scene anticipates *2 Henry VI*, in which justice itself becomes the central motif; in its emphasis upon the ceremonial aspects of adjudication, however, it serves as a variation on the dominant theme of Part I.

The Parliament scene draws together into a ceremonial design relationships that are established in the first two acts. The Winchester-Gloucester feud, having already broken into violence before the Tower of London, bursts into new fury as the quarreling of the disputants is interrupted by a skirmish of their

[33] Gordon, pp. 60-61.

servingmen—a social extension of aristocratic disorder which looks forward to the Cade rebellion in Part II. The altercation ends in a makeshift ritual as the two nobles are persuaded to shake hands publicly, a "token" that Gloucester hopes will serve "for a flag of truce / Betwixt ourselves and all our followers" (III.i.138-39). Their pledge is accepted naively by Henry, skeptically by Gloucester, not at all by Winchester, whose hypocrisy is revealed sotto voce to the audience. The scene's next ceremonial action, the reinstating of Plantagenet, is equally hollow: Plantagenet's humble oath of obedience is ironically undermined by the contrary vows made previously, after his interview with the dying Mortimer; and Somerset's aside—"Perish, base Prince, ignoble Duke of York" (l. 178)—offers a discordant reminder of the divisions sealed in the Temple Garden. As in all the major scenes, the emblematic action is reenforced by explicit didacticism. While the court exits to prepare for France, Exeter remains to voice his anxiety:

> Ay, we may march in England, or in France,
> Not seeing what is likely to ensue.
> This late dissension grown betwixt the peers
> Burns under feigned ashes of forg'd love,
> And will at last break out into a flame;
> As fester'd members rot but by degree
> Till bones and flesh and sinews fall away,
> So will this base and envious discord breed.
>
> [III.i.187-94]

The point at which the motif of ceremony receives its most sophisticated and complex elaboration occurs, appropriately enough, at Henry's coronation in Paris. The scene opens at the very moment of the crowning, an action ironically executed in consort by Gloucester and Winchester. Next Falstaff bursts in, only to be met by Talbot's furious assertions of knightly ideals, his subsequent degartering (itself an inverted ritual) and banishment. With Falstaff's exit, Gloucester opens the letter from Burgundy and glowers suspiciously at his breach of epistolary etiquette:

> What means his Grace, that he hath chang'd his style?
> No more but plain and bluntly "To the King"!
> Hath he forgot he is his sovereign?
> Or doth this churlish superscription
> Pretend some alteration in good-will?
>
> [IV.i.50-54]

Upon Talbot's departure to chastise Burgundy, Vernon and Basset fall out, followed by York and Somerset, whose altercation precipitates the scene's turning point—the king's misguided attempt

1 Henry VI: Chivalry and Ceremony

at reconciliation. Henry's crucial error, which contributes directly to the death of Talbot and all it signifies, is conceived of not only in political but in ceremonial terms. The king's political naiveté is of course apparent in his appointment of enemies to a joint command, but his utter indifference to the symbolic expressions of their hostility adds to this fault a different dimension. As he casually dons the red rose of Somerset, an act that cuts York to the quick, Henry remarks soothingly,

> I see no reason if I wear this rose,
> That any one should therefore be suspicious
> I more incline to Somerset than York:
> Both are my kinsmen, and I love them both;
> As well may they upbraid me with my crown
> Because, forsooth, the King of Scots is crown'd.
>
> [IV.i.152-57]

The basic modality of the scene makes it clear that this action represents not merely a high order of tactlessness but a sublime ignorance of the psychology of symbolism—an ignorance all the more astonishing in that it follows upon the contrary precedents of Gloucester and Talbot and of the king's own coronation. Shakespeare's handling of Henry in this scene is typical of the characterization throughout the tetralogy: characters are generally shaped with more regard to momentary thematic preoccupations than to psychological depth or coherence.

The conjunction of chivalric heroism and ceremonial mystique that unifies *1 Henry VI* represents an important tendency in Elizabethan thought, a tendency toward what Frances A. Yates calls an "imaginative re-feudalization of culture."[34] The most significant expressions of this attitude are Sidney's *Arcadia* and Spenser's *Faerie Queene,* but its manifestations were as often social as literary. Throughout her reign, for example, Elizabeth celebrated the anniversary of her accession, November 17, with a day of chivalric combats and spectacles. In 1590, probably the year in which *1 Henry VI* was first performed, Sir Henry Lee, who was said to have originated these accession day tilts, created a spectacular retirement ceremony attended by the queen and described in "Polyhymnia" by George Peele. Although bland enough in its own right, Peele's celebration of the encounter between Lee and the earl of Cumberland conveys better than any summary the peculiar impact of these anachronistic ceremonial occasions:

---

[34] "Elizabethan Chivalry: The Romance of the Accession Day Tilts," *Journal of the Warburg and Courtauld Institutes,* 20 (1957), 22.

> Mightie in Armes, mounted on puissant horse,
> Knight of the Crown in rich imbroderie,
> And costlie faire Caparison charg'd with Crownes,
> Oreshadowed with a withered running Vine,
> As who would say, My spring of youth is past:
> In Corslet gylt of curious workmanship,
> Sir Henry Lea, redoubted man at Armes
> Leades in the troopes, whom woorthie Cumberland
> Thrice noble Earle, aucutred as became
> So greate a Warriour and so good a Knight.
> Encountred first, yclad in coate of steele,
> And plumes and pendants al as white as Swanne,
> And speare in rest, right readie to performe
> What long'd unto the honour of the place.
> Together went these Champions, horse and man,
> Thundring along the Tylt, that at the shocke
> The hollow gyring vault of heaven resoundes.

At the conclusion of the tilting, in which thirteen couples participated, Lee resigned his place of honor to the earl of Cumberland in an elaborate ceremony before the queen. Peele renders her response and that of the assembled onlookers:

> Whereat she smiles, and sighes, and seem'd to say
> *Good Woodman, though thy greene be turn'd to gray,*
> *Thy age past Aprils prime, and pleasant May:*
> *Have thy request, we take him at thy praise,*
> *May he succeed the honour of thy daies.*
> Amen, said all, and hope they doo no lesse,
> No lesse his vertue and nobilitie,
> His skill in Armes and practise promiseth,
> And many Champions such may England live to have
> And daies and yeares as many such, as she in heart can crave.

Among the participants that day were Fulke Greville and the earl of Essex, the latter "Yclad in mightie Armes of mourners hue" in memory of Sir Philip Sidney, who had died four years before.[35] As Yates concludes, it is clear that "though feudalism as a working social or military structure was extinct, its forms were still the vehicle of living emotions."[36]

Through the motif of ceremony, then, Shakespeare creates out of the shapeless mass of the chronicles dramatic patterns with a special aesthetic and moral significance for his contemporaries. The universalizing tendencies of this dramatic method account for the wild departures from history, which prompt Geoffrey

---

[35] *The Life and Minor Works of George Peele*, ed. David H. Horne (New Haven, 1952), pp. 232-33, 242-43, 235.
[36] Yates, p. 22.

1 Henry VI: Chivalry and Ceremony

Bullough to call *1 Henry VI* "a fantasia on historical themes."[37] That similar tendencies characterize the best of Elizabethan history plays is argued convincingly by A. P. Rossiter in his preface to *Woodstock*. Stressing the influence of the morality tradition on the development of the genre, Rossiter coins the phrase " 'Moral History' " as "a useful name for history-plays where the shadow-show of a greater drama of state plays continually behind the human characters, sometimes (as in Shakespeare) upon something as large as the cyclorama of the stars."[38] *1 Henry VI* is similarly allegorical in method. What is most remarkable about the play in the context of the whole tetralogy, however, is the extent to which it embodies something of the uniqueness of a particular historical period. The world of *1 Henry VI*, though its truths are of all time, is distinctly a world in time. What one experiences in this play, as the unfolding of the tetralogy makes increasingly clear, are the earliest stages of social disintegration. The concept of ceremony, exalting as it does a vision of a social order in perfect balance, achieved for a brief moment under Henry V, serves as a static ideal against which the process of social decay is measured. In the "unkind division" of *1 Henry VI* Shakespeare defines an original sin that grows like a cancer until its final dissolution at the end of the tetralogy:

> As fester'd members rot but by degree
> Till bones and flesh and sinews fall away,
> So will this base and envious discord breed.
> [III.i.192-94]

That the ceremonial mode of *1 Henry VI* creates such a historical dimension cannot be appreciated without the benefit of hindsight; one's vision of historical process sharpens in focus with each step through the tetralogy. Something of the nature of this process can be perceived, however, by comparing perhaps the most elaborately ceremonial scene in the play—the Temple Garden episode (II.iv)—with the wars that ensue. If one compares the stylized ritual of selecting roses with any of the battles in Part III, or Plantagenet and Somerset with any of their progeny, what seems most striking is the disputants' mannered self-control. The ritual of the roses, of course, stands in ironic relationship to Talbot's chivalric ideal: it evolves out of a legal impasse; its terms are broken as soon as they are agreed upon; its very existence—as an ad hoc ceremony—is a contradiction in terms. At the same time that it depicts a perversion of true ceremony, however, the episode

---

[37] *Narrative and Dramatic Sources of Shakespeare*, III (New York, 1960), 25.
[38] *Woodstock* (London, 1946), p. 9.

exemplifies in the broader context of the tetralogy the extent to which the old forms, though increasingly emptied of content, continue to survive. In contrast to what they and their descendants will become in time, these nobles are neither scheming villains nor bloodthirsty warriors; they grasp instinctively, it seems, for the saving forms of social order. Their ceremoniousness, though perverse and misguided, testifies to their compulsion to define themselves within the framework of a community. In *1 Henry VI* all roads return to Talbot's meeting with the Countess of Auvergne.

After the death of Talbot in Act IV, the play moves somewhat fitfully to its ominous but inconclusive end. Gestures are made toward continuity in the ceremonial quality of Henry's contract to marry the daughter of the earl of Armagnac (he sends as "pledge" a jewel); in the seductive witchcraft passed from the dying Joan to Margaret of Anjou; in the persistence of English dissension and French treachery. But for the most part Shakespeare seems to have his eyes upon the central concerns of the next play. He underplays the ironies in York's taunting of Joan—one would like to see Somerset in that scene as well, since it so naturally parallels the death of Talbot—and concentrates instead on sketches preliminary to Part II: of Suffolk's infatuation for Margaret, of York's rancor at the French peace, of Gloucester's judicious opposition to the proposed marriage, of Henry's naive disregard of the responsibilities of power. Although such anticipations stand somewhat awkwardly outside the central concerns of *1 Henry VI*, they are necessary to the development of the tetralogy as a whole. Unlike the mature histories, the *Henry VI* plays suffer considerably if performed or read in isolation.

2 *Henry VI:* Justice and Law

In *1 Henry VI* the initial stages of England's social disintegration after the death of Henry V are portrayed in a dramatic mode dependent upon the combined themes of chivalry and ceremony; in *2 Henry VI* the ensuing stages are articulated through the concepts of justice and the law. The extensiveness and subtlety of these new thematic variations provide evidence of Shakespeare's increasing dramatic maturity. Humphrey of Gloucester, whom Hall describes as "very well learned in the lawe civill, detestyng malefactors, and punishyng their offences,"[1] serves as a virtual personification of the law, much as Talbot embodies the values of chivalry in Part I. But the theme extends well beyond his symbolic role, permeating all of the major episodes of the play with a remarkable variety of legal terms and procedures. We see, for example, the right of petition exercised (though fruitlessly) by the commoners before Suffolk and the queen; a trial by combat in the case of Peter the apprentice and his master, Horner; the trial and banishment of the duchess of Gloucester; an ad hoc adjudication of the "miracle" of Saint Albans; a claim to the throne based on genealogical argument; preparations, at least, for a trial of the Lord Protector; a civil insurrection aimed at overturning all rule of law; open rebellion. As in the case of ceremony in Part I, the concept of law serves as a method of characterization, a mode of dramatic action, a measure of social and political decay.[2]

Like ceremony, the notion of rule by law lies at the center of Elizabethan social thought. Divine in origin, law is both symbol and cause of order, creator and sustainer of civilization. In his famous peroration to Book I of *The Laws of Ecclesiastical Polity,* Richard Hooker offers a personification comparable in conception and rhetorical grandeur to Chapman's goddess, Ceremony: "of Law there can be no less acknowledged, than that her seat is the

---

[1] See *Narrative and Dramatic Sources of Shakespeare,* ed. Geoffrey Bullough, III (London, 1960), 107.

[2] For a complementary, though more limited, analysis of the theme of law, see Don M. Ricks, *Shakespeare's Emergent Form: A Study of the Structures of the* Henry VI *Plays,* Monograph Series, XV, No. 1 (Logan: Utah State University Press, June 1968), pp. 70-73.

bosom of God, her voice the harmony of the world: all things in heaven and earth do her homage, the very least as feeling her care, and the greatest as not exempted from her power: both Angels and men and creatures of what condition soever, though each in different sort and manner, yet all with uniform consent, admiring her as the mother of their peace and joy."[3] Even more pertinent to *2 Henry VI* is Thomas Elyot's emphatic assertion of the value of justice in *The Governor*: "The most excellent and incomparable virtue called justice is so necessary and expedient for the governor of a public weal that without it none other virtue may be commendable, nor wit or any manner of doctrine profitable."[4] Elyot's insistence upon the radical importance of justice does much to explain the nature of Gloucester's role as good governor and the symbolic significance of his death.

The opening moments of *2 Henry VI,* like those of Part I, introduce an action that serves as an emblem for the play as a whole; Part I begins with a disrupted funeral ceremony, Part II with the interrupted reading of a marriage contract. The scene commences with a flourish of trumpets, hautboys, and the ceremonial entrance of the king and his assembled nobles. Suffolk, in a speech designed to recall ironically the obeisance of Talbot, formally relinquishes his proxy title to the queen:

> In presence of the Kings of France and Sicil,
> The Dukes of Orleans, Calabar, Bretagne, Alencon,
> Seven earls, twelve barons, and twenty reverend bishops,
> I have performed my task, and was espous'd:
> And humbly now upon my bended knee,
> In sight of England and her lordly peers,
> Deliver up my title in the Queen
> To your gracious hands, that are the substance
> Of that great shadow I did represent. . . .
>
> [I.i.6-14][5]

The roll call of titles, the humble kneeling, the play on substance and shadow (the means by which Talbot defined his loyalty to the king) are for this decadent aristocrat merely the empty forms of courtly ritual. Suffolk's dissembled allegiance is followed by a greeting between the king and queen, after which the nobles kneel together and exclaim to a flourish, "Long live Queen Margaret, England's happiness!" (l. 37). With the reading of the "articles of contracted peace," however, the unity of the occasion breaks apart; as Gloucester reads of the loss of Anjou and Maine,

[3] *Of the Laws of Ecclesiastical Polity* (London, 1907), I, 232.
[4] Ed. S. E. Lehmberg (London, 1962), p. 159.
[5] All citations to *2 Henry VI* are from the Arden edition of Andrew S. Cairncross (London, 1962).

2 Henry VI: Justice and Law

he suddenly lets fall the parchment—"Some sudden qualm hath struck me at the heart / And dimm'd mine eyes that I can read no further" (ll. 54-55). Cardinal Winchester, who suffers no such misgivings, continues the reading. After creating Suffolk a duke for his efforts, Henry departs in order to prepare for the coronation of his queen. Once he has left, Gloucester vents his anguish at the proceedings and is joined in expressions of outrage by the other nobles. Even the unanimity of protest is short lived, however, and dissolves into factionalism and intrigue. As Gloucester exits, the cardinal stirs up opposition against him; as the cardinal leaves, Buckingham and Somerset express their hostility toward both parties; as they depart, Salisbury, Warwick, and York remain to vow allegiance to Gloucester; finally, York is left alone to voice his own ambition for the throne. The departures are meticulously choreographed, creating a vivid image of social dissension. The scene's chief symbol, the legal parchment dropped to the floor, lingers in the mind; the marriage contract is of no substance, either as a private or public document.

The origin of the contract, as is displayed in Part I, lies in Henry's Petrarchan susceptibility to Suffolk's eloquent descriptions of Margaret. In this scene, however, in a shift that betrays the thematic preoccupations of the tetralogy, Henry's Petrarchism becomes piety, the trait that is to characterize him throughout the play:

> O Lord, that lends me life,
> Lend me a heart replete with thankfulness!
> For thou hast given me in this beauteous face
> A world of earthly blessings to my soul,
> If sympathy of love unite our thoughts.
>
> [I.i.19-23]

In Part I Henry's puerile amorousness blinds him to the nature of his public responsibility; in Part II his piety does the same. Although the new conception in no sense contradicts the old, it does not provide the consistency of psychological development one comes to expect in the later histories, as in the case of Bolingbroke, for example, or Falstaff. The relative unconcern for continuity of character typified in Shakespeare's treatment of Henry is indicative of his early dramatic priorities.[6]

---

[6]Modern critics are sometimes guilty of a misdirected search for psychological development in the characterization of these plays. Although he does not consider Henry's shift in character, Robert Ornstein treats Gloucester and Margaret as examples of Shakespeare's concern for psychological evolution. Gloucester, who shows no signs of being a figurehead of the law in Part I, is characterized by Ornstein as "a somewhat older and wiser man in Part II," as if his new orientation were simply the result of maturity (*A Kingdom for a Stage* [Cambridge, Mass., 1972], p.43).

Throughout the play Henry's piety takes the form of what might be called "providentialism"—an exaggerated belief in the active intervention of divine judgment in human affairs. It manifests itself, therefore, in a form peculiarly suited to the play's dominant motifs of justice and the law. The news of the "miracle" of Saint Albans, for example, prompts Henry to instantaneous and ill-conceived rejoicing: "Now, God be prais'd, that to believing souls / Gives light in darkness, comfort in despair!" (II.i.66-67). Gloucester's exposure of the fraud, though it jolts Henry into another pious ejaculation—"O God! seest Thou this, and bearest so long?" (l. 147)—awakens no new insight, for he betrays the same pious optimism only moments later upon the announcement of the duchess of Gloucester's arrest: "O God! what mischief work the wicked ones, / Heaping confusion on their own heads thereby!" (ll. 178-79). Only slightly less ironic is Henry's attitude toward the victory of Peter over his master in trial by combat:

> Go, take hence that traitor from our sight;
> For by his death we do perceive his guilt:
> And God in justice hath reveal'd to us
> The truth and innocence of this poor fellow. . . .
>
> [II.iii.97-100]

Law is for Henry, then, above all the law of God, executed directly and unambiguously in earthly judgments. Gloucester's skepticism provides a foil for Henry's navieté in the Saint Albans scene, while York's reaction to the victory of Peter, cynical though it may be, meets more accurately than Henry's the event's implications: "Fellow, thank God, and the good wine in thy master's way" (II.iii.92). It is important to notice, however, that Henry's providential perspective, though dangerously limited, is not totally discredited; York's cynicism has its own limitations, and the fates of Winchester and Suffolk offer evidence enough that divine retribution is a contingency to be reckoned with. To see as Henry does the hand of God everywhere at work, however, is to fall prey to a credulity akin to superstition. As Canterbury observes in *Henry V*,

> miracles are ceas'd;
> And therefore we must needs admit the means
> How things are perfected.
>
> [I.i.67-69]

Henry's "providentialism," moreover, is ethically debilitating, for his dependence on God's justice prevents him from asserting himself in positive action. When Somerset announces the loss of all the French territories, the king laments, "Cold news, Lord Somerset: but God's will be done!" (III.i.86). And when in the

2 Henry VI: Justice and Law

same scene the nobles levy their fraudulent charges against Gloucester, Henry accedes to their lawlessness as a passive victim:

> And as the dam runs lowing up and down,
> Looking the way her harmless young ones went,
> And can do naught but wail her darling's loss;
> Even so myself bewails good Gloucester's case
> With sad unhelpful tears, and with dimm'd eyes
> Look after him, and cannot do him good;
> So mighty are his vowed enemies.
>
> [III.i.214-20]

Gloucester's enemies may be mighty, but Henry is king; in view of his consistent providential outlook, moreover, it seems likely that his pathetic helplessness derives more from his belief that Gloucester is the victim of a "low'ring star" (l. 206) than from any fear of the nobles. Although Henry is stung into self-assertion at the murder of Gloucester, both by his own moral outrage and the newfound support of the commoners, to the point that he actually banishes Suffolk, he soon relapses into his former inertness. He is last seen on the field at Saint Albans, exasperating Margaret by his refusal to retreat, an exemplum neither of valor nor of cowardice but of paralysis induced by an obsession with providential judgment: "Can we outrun the heavens? Good Margaret, stay" (V.ii.73-74).

In many ways Henry VI seems a preliminary sketch for the vastly richer and more complicated figure of Richard II. Henry's exaggerated dependence on divine intervention is echoed in Richard's rather more egocentric response to Bolingbroke's rebellion upon his landing in Wales:

> For every man that Bolingbroke hath press'd
> To lift shrewd steel against our golden crown,
> God for his Richard hath in heavenly pay
> A glorious angel. . . .
>
> [III.ii.58-61]

Here the analysis of the providential vision is more sharply focused and complex, pointing at once to a precise political doctrine, that of divine right, and to the psychological imbalance that presses it to such extremes. Carlisle's objection to Richard's earlier conjuration of the earth, moreover, provides an appropriate gloss for Henry's inaction at Saint Albans:

> Fear not, my lord; that Power that made you king
> Hath power to keep you king in spite of all.
> The means that heavens yield must be embrac'd,
> And not neglected.
>
> [III.ii.27-30]

The naive belief that, as Richard puts it, "Heaven still guards the right" (l. 62) thus prompts both kings to abjure their own responsibilities, to succumb to a sense of deterministic inertia. In retrospect there seems as well in Henry's passivity at Saint Albans a hint of the melancholy that leads Richard at such moments of crisis to yearn for annihilation: "Beshrew thee, cousin, which didst lead me forth / Of that sweet way I was in to despair!" (ll. 204-5).

Although Henry's role grows more important and more intriguing as the tetralogy unfolds, in Part II he hovers on the fringes of the dramatic action. As the opening scene foreshadows, it is Gloucester and York who dominate the attention of the audience; indeed, as has often been observed, the play is structured upon the reversal in their respective fortunes. During the first half York bides his time, helping in the arrest of the duchess and justifying his claim to the throne to Warwick and Salisbury, while the queen, Winchester, and Suffolk seize the initiative and undermine Gloucester through betrayal and false accusation. Immediately after the nobles conspire to murder the Lord Protector, York, in soliloquy, determines to make his move. The action reaches a climax in Act II, Scene ii, when Gloucester's corpse is presented at his trial. The remainder of the play works out the consequences of Gloucester's downfall, in the grisly deaths of Winchester and Suffolk and in the rise of York, first through the Cade rebellion, which he has fomented, and finally through his victory in the first battle of the civil wars at Saint Albans. Though still loose-knit by the standards of the mature histories, the play's structure marks a distinct advance in clarity over that of Part I. Its dependence upon the contrasting patterns of its protagonists suggests another connection with *Richard II*.

Like Bolingbroke and Richard, York and Gloucester are opposed in nature as well as fortune. The two dominant speeches of the opening scene epitomize the conflict in values and temperaments that determines the shape of the play. Upon the exit of the king, Gloucester's pent-up anguish explodes:

> Brave peers of England, pillars of the state,
> To you Duke Humphrey must unload his grief—
> Your grief, the common grief of all the land.
>
> [I.i.74-76]

Recapitulating the former glories and hardships of conquering and holding France, he concludes with a bitter denunciation of the terms of the marriage:

> Shall Henry's conquest, Bedford's vigilance,
> Your deeds of war, and all our counsel die?

> O peers of England! shameful is this league,
> Fatal this marriage, cancelling your fame,
> Blotting your names from books of memory,
> Razing the characters of your renown,
> Defacing monuments of conquer'd France,
> Undoing all, as all had never been!
>
> [I.i.95-102]

As the rhetoric reveals, in its gestures toward the common good, toward heroic valor and eternal fame, Gloucester represents a continuation of the ideals earlier embodied in Talbot; Gloucester's heroism, however, manifests itself in civil, rather than martial, virtue.

York at first joins the chorus of complaints provoked by Gloucester's indignation and later, after the departures of Winchester, Buckingham, and Somerset, supports Salisbury and Warwick in their vow to stand by the Lord Protector as long as his deeds "tend the profit of the land" (I.i.205). York immediately disengages himself from these patriots, however, first in an aside, then in soliloquy:

> Anjou and Maine are given to the French;
> Paris is lost; the state of Normandy
> Stands on a tickle point now they are gone;
> Suffolk concluded on the articles,
> The peers agreed, and Henry was well pleas'd
> To change two dukedoms for a duke's fair daughter.
> I cannot blame them all: what is't to them?
> 'Tis thine they give away, and not their own.
> Pirates may make cheap pennyworths of their pillage,
> And purchase friends, and give to courtezans,
> Still revelling like lords till all be gone;
> While as the silly owner of the goods
> Weeps over them, and wrings his hapless hands,
> And shakes his head, and trembling stands aloof,
> While all is shar'd and all is borne away,
> Ready to starve, and dare not touch his own.
> So York must sit and fret and bite his tongue
> While his own lands are bargain'd for and sold.
>
> [I.i.215-32]

The interplay between Gloucester's public protest and this private indignation creates resonances that linger throughout the work. York shares Gloucester's hostility to the French marriage, of course, but the terms of their patriotism are radically opposed. For Gloucester the loss of Anjou and Maine is one not of land but of honor; in "undoing all, as all had never been," Henry's "shameful league" has consigned to oblivion the heroic efforts of the English nobility dead and living. For York, however, the loss of the territories represents merely a loss of property; "two dukedoms for a duke's fair daughter" is a bad bargain. (It is no coincidence, one suspects, that a similarly playful alliteration occurs in Shylock's "my ducats and my daughter.") York conceives of the property, moreover, as personal real estate; he sees himself sardonically as "the silly owner of the goods." Even a less reductive metaphor would not vindicate York's conception of the lands, for the king himself has no proprietary rights; in *Richard II* John of Gaunt is outraged that Richard has leased out the realm "like to a tenement or pelting farm" (II.i.60). The contrast between the two speeches lies not merely in principle but in personality as well; with a naturalness beyond the scope of *1 Henry VI,* the psychology of the speakers complements their opposing values. Gloucester operates in public, with an impulsive, passionate concern for the common good; York in secret, with a cool, caustic attention to his own self-interest—"I cannot blame them all: what is't to them?" He is, after all, the father of Richard III.

When compared to his counterpart, Talbot in *1 Henry VI,* Humphrey, duke of Gloucester seems a remarkably complicated and richly human protagonist. Like Talbot, however, he fulfills an emblematic role—one that is most precisely defined, in fact, in an episode analogous to the Countess of Auvergne scene in Part I. The "miracle" of Saint Albans, like Talbot's visit to the Countess, creates a complex perspective on the hero and the values he embodies. The scene begins with a series of biting exchanges between Gloucester and Winchester, provoked by Henry's innocent moralization of the high pitch of Gloucester's falcon; within moments the two opponents have secretly arranged a duel. At this point the Mayor of Saint Albans enters with others bearing Simpcox in a chair. Simpcox tells of the miraculous recovery of his sight, only to be tricked by Gloucester into disproving his former blindness (he is able to name colors) and his supposed lameness (he leaps over a stool at the prompting of the Beadle's whip). The scene ends on a solemn note, with Gloucester's sorrow at the announcement of his wife's arrest and the king's command to return to London for the trial.

Although rooted in folklore—compare the judgment of Solomon—the Simpcox episode derives from a source as contemporary as John Foxe; in *Acts and Monuments* Foxe celebrates the shrewd debunking of the "miracle" as proof that "Duke Humfrey had not onely an head to disserne and dissever trueth from forged and fayned hipocrisie, but study also and diligence lykewise was in him, to reforme that which was amisse."⁷ Foxe's observation seems to have provided the germinal idea for Gloucester's role throughout the play. In this scene, moreover, Shakespeare fleshes out the description by the inclusion of dramatic foils whose attitudes and actions counter Humphrey's: Henry, whose naive piety prevents him from discerning the truth, and Margaret, Suffolk, and Winchester, whose "study" at the moment is not social reform but the baiting of Gloucester and the betrayal of his duchess. Gloucester thus emerges as the mean between a piety that blurs vision and a "policy" that misdirects action.

To Foxe's skeletal narration of the Simpcox episode Shakespeare adds as well a preface (the challenge) and a conclusion (the news of the duchess's arrest); the effect of both is to create complicating perspectives on Gloucester—perspectives subtler and more varied than those offered in the analogue of Talbot's interview with the Countess of Auvergne. In view of Gloucester's role as a representative of the law, it seems incongruous to modern sensibilities to find him preparing for a duel; it would have seemed abhorrent, no doubt, to some Elizabethans. Yet there is little question that the dramatic situation depends upon a popular opinion ready to support him in the defense of his honor; Winchester's direct challenge and added insults cannot be honorably ignored. Sir Philip Sidney, after all, sprang to the defense of his good name in similar circumstances when humiliated on the tennis courts by the earl of Oxford.⁸ The impetuosity with which Gloucester rises to the occasion, moreover, adds a further dimension to the otherwise bland role of good governor. It is with a similar impulsive passion that Gloucester drops the marriage contract in the play's opening scene and on a later occasion leaves the palace rather than endure the insults of the nobles, to return only after his choler is "overblown / With walking once about the quadrangle..." (I.iii.152-53). Throughout the play Gloucester's passion is righteous, open, honestly eccentric, an endearing contrast to the wily self-control of his opponents. The terrible irony of the dueling exchange lies in the audience's immediate awareness of the limitations of that openness. In the preceding scene Gloucester's duchess has been arrested; the honor he

---

⁷Bullough, III, 128.

⁸For the strength of Elizabethan popular support of dueling, see Ruth Kelso, who cites the Sidney-Oxford encounter, *The Doctrine of the English Gentleman in the Sixteenth Century*, University of Illinois Studies in Language and Literature, XIV, Nos. 1-2 (Feb.-May, 1929), pp. 101-2; see also Fredson T. Bowers, *Elizabethan Revenge Tragedy* (Princeton, 1940), pp. 30-34.

prepares to defend has been in one sense already lost. "Protector, see to't well, protect yourself," threatens the cardinal (II.i.55). Though empty words when applied to Gloucester's swordsmanship or courage, the duchess's downfall fills them with an ominous meaning.

The ironic undertones that pervade the beginning of the scene deepen with the announcement of the duchess's arrest at its end. While Gloucester has been hawking, the cardinal's men have been stalking other game; while Gloucester has been proving himself firm in the support of his personal honor and both wise and just in his prosecution of public law, his wife has been proving his defenselessness against the snares of his enemies. The ironies pass over Gloucester, of course. Sure in his virtue and respect for the law, he betrays neither fear for his own safety nor excessive pity for the predicament of his wife:

> Noble she is, but if she have forgot
> Honour and virtue, and convers'd with such
> As, like to pitch, defile nobility,
> I banish her my bed and company,
> And give her as a prey to law and shame,
> That hath dishonour'd Gloucester's honest name.
>
> [II.i.186-91]

That he regards her as "a prey to law and shame" (the metaphor rounds off the hawking motif) heightens the ironies of his stoic resolution. With a faith unnervingly akin to Henry's, though more secular in its orientation, he will accompany the king to London to "poise the cause in Justice' equal scales, / Whose beam stands sure, whose rightful cause prevails" (ll.196-97).

As an epitome of the good governor, the Lord Protector bases his life upon the concept of justice and derives his strength from an abiding faith in the process of law. Without justice, says Elyot, as we have observed, "none other virtue may be commendable, nor wit or any manner of doctrine profitable." It is this faith that enables Gloucester to chide his duchess for her ambitious thoughts, resign her without murmur to trial, acquiesce with patience in her open penance and banishment: "Eleanor, the law, thou seest, hath judged thee: / I cannot justify whom the law condemns" (II.iii.15-16). Even in the face of his wife's warnings against the machinations of Suffolk, York, and Winchester, he remains unmoved:

> Ah! Nell, forbear: thou aimest all awry;
> I must offend before I be attainted;
> And had I twenty times so many foes,

2 Henry VI: Justice and Law

> And each of them had twenty times their power,
> All these could not procure me any scathe,
> So long as I am loyal, true, and crimeless.
>
> [II.iv.58-63]

Although analogous to Henry's belief in God's justice, Gloucester's faith is not equally naive; the Saint Albans episode, after all, is designed to display his shrewdness. As becomes apparent when he is accused, moreover, Gloucester's refusal to swerve from the course of law is not based on ignorance of the plots against him:

> Ay, all of you have laid your heads together—
> Myself had notice of your conventicles—
> And all to make away my guiltless life.
>
> [III.i.165-67]

Instead, it is based upon an unyielding, uncompromising allegiance to moral virtue. Such an allegiance, of course, even when the law supports it, cannot prevent murder; nor can it preserve the commonweal from the threat of those for whom the rule of law is a meaningless phrase.

The qualities he exemplifies and the ultimate ineffectuality of his stance combine to place Gloucester within a remarkably cohesive though short-lived stage tradition of the good governor. The unbending moral probity, the steadfast allegiance to the law, even the impulsive anger of Gloucester are shared both by Thomas of Woodstock in the anonymous play *Woodstock* and by John of Gaunt in *Richard II*. Both characters are given to passionate outbursts, Woodstock in response to the baiting of the king and courtiers on his new clothes (I.iii) and Gaunt in his deathbed denunciation of Richard's abuses (II.i). Woodstock in particular exhibits some of Gloucester's endearing eccentricity, to the point of preferring plain old English frieze—he is called "plain Thomas"—to attire more appropriate for his exalted status as Lord Protector. In his preface to the play, A. P. Rossiter comments perceptively on the essential values that tie Woodstock to Gloucester: "What they represent is England, seen very englishly as an insulated stand of manly virtue, where the good man is simple, direct, unsuspicious, public-spirited, and good-humored if not a humorist; where a mixture of shrewdness and forthrightness is preferred to cleverness, and a man can be firm to what he sees as right, though the worldly moral be no better than Juvenal's 'Probitas laudatur, et alget.' "[9] The remarkable family resemblances among all three characters testify to the central role the

---

[9] *Woodstock* (London, 1946), p. 66.

concept of the good governor played in the Elizabethan imagination. The most crucial trait they exemplify is of course the most problematic—an unwillingness to compromise moral virtue for personal or public expediency. Gloucester knowingly martyrs himself to the law; Woodstock, who refuses time and again to rebel against his lawful king, despite countless injustices, does likewise (he is murdered while writing a letter of advice to Richard); and John of Gaunt, though not murdered, dies with an unyielding faith in the doctrine of passive resistance, which in the world of the play expires with him.

The problem posed by these figures is one central to the political consciousness of the period: how, in a corrupt society ineptly ruled, can a virtuous man contribute to his own or the greater good? For audiences accustomed to a pervasive moral relativism this problem tends to evaporate: one must bend a bit to the winds of politics, be pragmatic, sacrifice a little of the means for the sake of the end. But for most Elizabethans, absolutists in theory if not in practice, the problem becomes truly a dilemma: to bend is to give implicit sanction to Machiavellianism. Figures like Gloucester and Woodstock, in fact, seem calculated to put to the test traditional Elizabethan abhorrence for Machiavelli's dictum "Hee who leaves that which is done, for that which ought to bee done, learnes sooner his ruine, than his preservation."[10]

The discomfort we may feel at the ineffectuality of these characters derives, it seems, from an instinctive distrust of the absolutist positions Machiavelli was the first to challenge; to understand the tragic impact of their deaths, one must hold such instincts in suspension. This is not to say, of course, that the plays do no more than body forth the commonplace assumptions of the age. Quite the contrary. The fate of Gloucester, like that of Woodstock or Gaunt, compels one to grapple with the challenging implications of a moralistic stance: failure to compromise leads, more often than not, to personal ruin and political disorder. Such a tragic vision is at a far remove from the assumptions of Elizabethan political moralists like Elyot, who were prone to stress a direct connection between virtue and political success. Amyot's famous Preface to *Plutarch's Lives* spells out this viewpoint with a frankness almost embarrassing: "If you first set your selfe in order, and then dispose all other things according to vertue, all things shall fall out according to your desire."[11] Although

---

[10] *Nicholas Machiavel's Prince*, tr. E[dward] D[acres] (London, 1640), p. 118.

[11] *The Lives of the Noble Grecians and Romans*, tr. Thomas North (London, 1579), sig. vi^v.

2 Henry VI: Justice and Law

Elizabethan dramatists never openly advocated the opposite remedy, as Machiavelli came perilously close to doing, through figures like Gloucester, Woodstock, and Gaunt they countered the pious optimism of some humanists with their own tragic perceptions.

Gloucester's death, like Talbot's, is personally heroic and publicly shameful, a martyrdom for a principle no one else in the society upholds. Just as Talbot's death symbolizes the end of the chivalric conception of community, Gloucester's marks the expiration of rule by law—though the latter substitutes the brutality of murder for the elegiac calm of Talbot's dying union with his son. The play's emotional climax occurs, appropriately enough, in a court of law, when Warwick draws aside the curtain to reveal Gloucester's corpse and with this simple motion transforms a trial into an inquest:

> But see, his face is black and full of blood,
> His eye-balls further out than when he liv'd,
> Staring full ghastly like a strangled man;
> His hair uprear'd, his nostrils stretch'd with struggling;
> His hands abroad display'd, as one that grasp'd
> And tugged for life, and was by strength subdu'd.
>
> [III.ii.167-72]

Though Gloucester's soul, like Talbot's, presumably wings its way to heaven, Shakespeare's stress on the grisly details of the murder and its grotesque consequences reflects a new ironic intensity that will darken as the tetralogy unfolds. Confronted with the murder of its defendant, the court comes to terms with the situation in a grim mockery of justice. Henry, though heartbroken and suspicious of foul play, is paralyzed by the anxiety of rendering false judgment: "If my suspect be false, forgive me, God, / For judgment only doth belong to Thee" (ll. 138-39). With profoundly expressive inaction, he cannot bring himself to view the circumstantial evidence of the corpse. Warwick and Salisbury, though they press to the attack against Suffolk, do so for less than noble reasons, having previously agreed to aid York in his attempt to secure the throne.[12] That only the lawless mob of threatening commoners can spur Henry to action affords the final irony of the scene. The banishment of Suffolk, a haphazard judgment at best, is the first of a series of acts in which law and justice are turned on end.

---

[12] For a convincing analysis of the motives of Salisbury and Warwick in this scene, see Ornstein, p. 48.

The two chief movers of Gloucester's death, Winchester and Suffolk, are subjected to judgments darkly appropriate to their own deviousness, judgments both extralegal and extraordinary. Winchester, mysteriously struck down, writhes with a tormented conscience and, with a materialism nicely ironic in a cardinal, tries to buy off death:

> If thou be'st death, I'll give thee England's treasure,
> Enough to purchase such another island,
> So thou wilt let me live, and feel no pain.
>
> [III.iii.2-4]

Henry, looking on, but with his vision focused on the Day of Judgment, responds for once in a manner called forth by the occasion: "Forbear to judge, for we are sinners all" (l. 31). As evidence that the dreadful solemnity of the scene can be emotionally compelling, we have the powerful reaction of Samuel Johnson: "These are beauties that rise out of nature and of truth; the superficial reader cannot miss them, the profound can image nothing beyond them."[13] Suffolk, in a scene that also hints at providential mysteries, perishes at the hands of the pirate, Walter—a death foreshadowed in Gloucester's prophetic dream. He also dies unrepentant, though with the preoccupations of a decadent aristocrat rather than those of a corrupt churchman:

> It is impossible that I should die
> By such a lowly vassal as thyself.
> Thy words move rage and not remorse in me.
>
> [IV.i.109-11]

In Suffolk's case justice is executed in a mock trial that parodies Gloucester's. Blatantly disregarding verisimilitude, Shakespeare fashions his pirates into a court of inquiry, the lieutenant's harangue into a verdict from the bench:

> Ay, kennel, puddle, sink, whose filth
> Troubles the silver spring where England drinks;
> Now will I dam up this thy yawning mouth
> For swallowing the treasure of the realm.
> Thy lips, that kiss'd the Queen, shall sweep the ground;
> And thou that smil'dst at good Duke Humphrey's death,
> Against the senseless winds shalt grin in vain. . . .
>
> [IV.i.70-76]

The lieutenant goes on to accuse Suffolk of contributing to the loss of France, the plots of Warwick, York, and the Nevils, and the

---

[13] *Johnson on Shakespeare*, ed. Arthur Sherbo, Yale Edition of the Works of Samuel Johnson, VIII (New Haven, 1968), 591.

2 Henry VI: Justice and Law

uprising of the commons in Kent. Suffolk's head ends in the hands of Margaret, who dandles it distractedly before the king, provoking a rare thrust of irony: "I fear me, love, if that I had been dead, / Thou wouldest not have mourn'd so much for me" (IV.iv.22-23). Like Richard II, Henry grows keener in insight but remains politically ineffectual.

With Gloucester's downfall, York begins his rise. Although defined primarily in terms of his relation to the themes of justice and the law, as are Henry and Gloucester, York is rendered with a new psychological complexity and coherence. Woven into the character are two dominant strains that determine not only the nature of his actions but the shape of his language: personal ambition and a belief in both his legal and natural rights to the throne. Both of these motives are intertwined in his opening soliloquy:

> A day will come when York shall claim his own;
> And therefore I will take the Nevils' parts
> And make a show of love to proud Duke Humphrey,
> And when I spy advantage, claim the crown,
> For that's the golden mark I seek to hit.
> Nor shall proud Lancaster usurp my right,
> Nor hold the sceptre in his childish fist,
> Nor wear the diadem upon his head,
> Whose church-like humour fits not for a crown.
>
> [I.i.240-48]

The ambition is obvious enough, though not so simple as Tillyard's reductive comment implies: "He is hardly human, and is more the simple embodiment of personal ambition."[14] The psychological underpinnings are rather complex. When York speaks of his right to the throne, it is often difficult to ascertain, as it is here, whether his reference is to rights of property ("claim his own") or of succession ("usurp my right") or of natural superiority ("childish fist," "church-like humour"). A similar conflation of concepts occurs in subtler form in his speech upon his return from Ireland:

> From Ireland thus comes York to claim his right,
> And pluck the crown from feeble Henry's head:
> Ring, bells, aloud; burn, bonfires, clear and bright,
> To entertain great England's lawful king.
> Ah! sancta majestas, who'd not buy thee dear?
> Let them obey that knows not how to rule;

---

[14]*Shakespeare's History Plays* (London, 1944), p. 214.

> This hand was made to handle nought but gold:
> I cannot give due action to my words,
> Except a sword or sceptre balance it.
> A sceptre shall it have, have I a sword,
> On which I'll toss the fleur-de-luce of France.
>
> [V.i.1-11]

In its supple combination of psychological and moral perspectives, the speech anticipates the more complicated characterization of the later histories. York's mind jumps from the question of right to that of power (ll. 1-2), then to the lawfulness of his title (l. 4)—as if plucking the crown from a feeble king constituted an act of law rather than force. His proprietary instincts emerge with the grotesquely indecorous desire to *buy* sancta majestas (l. 5), and remain to fill the word *gold* with mercenary significance until it slides imperceptibly into a sword of state. But then the ceremonial sword becomes the sword of force (ll. 9-10), the end and the means by this time totally confused. The impression created is one of a mind poised complacently on the edge of moral chaos.

York's legal claim to the throne, as is made clear by the dying Mortimer in Part I, has a basis firmer than mere hypocrisy. As he expounds it in his garden to Salisbury and Warwick, his title is technically sound: Henry's line extends from the fourth son of Edward III, York's from the third (II.ii). This is legitimacy enough, it seems, to convince Salisbury and Warwick, whose instincts up to this point have been on the side of right; in their susceptibility, perhaps, lies the germ of a later yielding, that of the duke of York to Bolingbroke in *Richard II* (II.iii). Though York's claim has at least a psychological validity that mitigates his crimes—he is no Richard III, merely his father—it has no true legal or moral basis whatever; the thrust of the garden scene makes this clear. It is possible, I suppose, to entertain the notion that to some members of an Elizabethan audience—a Selden, say, or a Stowe—the genealogical catalog that extends for a good fifty lines would have been comprehensible, but it is impossible to imagine the less initiated—and not necessarily the groundlings—responding to Warwick's conclusion with anything other than a mystified smile: "What plain proceedings is more plain than this?" (II.ii.52). The function of the scene is to pursue the motif of law into the realm of a pedantic legalism that betrays its essential values. Henry VI is a de facto king, in the direct line of succession of a house that has ruled for roughly fifty years; although weak, he is neither tyrant nor usurper. The Tudor doctrine of allegiance in this instance speaks common sense. Whatever sympathy may be

2 *Henry VI*: Justice and Law

generated by York's recital of his claim, moreover, is immediately dissipated by the nature of his plans to press it:

> We thank you, lords. But I am not your king
> Till I be crown'd and that my sword be stain'd
> With heart-blood of the house of Lancaster;
> And that's not suddenly to be perform'd
> But with advice and silent secrecy.
>
> [II.ii.63-67]

York is a victim of history, of course, but so is history of him.

York's belief in the rights of natural superiority makes him, like Edmund in *King Lear,* a threat to Elizabethan moral norms: "Let them obey that knows not how to rule" (V.i.6). With a more customary ambiguity, he proclaims himself "far better born than is the King, / More like a king, more kingly in my thoughts" (V.i.28-29)—evidence, he thinks, that justice demands his accession. In a society based on hierarchy and primogeniture, such a conception of natural law poses a severe danger—or, to the more venturesome, a dazzling opportunity. The recurrence of the motif in the literature of the period—in Marlowe, Daniel, Drayton— suggests the strength of its evocative power. When Elyot in *The Governor* envisages the prospect of a society without law, he describes a state of affairs that York implicitly endorses and in action brings into being: "without governance and laws the persons most strong in body should by violence constrain them that be of less strength and weaker to labour as bondmen or slaves for their sustenance and other necessaries, the strong men being without labour or care. Then were all our equality dashed, and finally as beasts savage the one shall desire to slay another."[15] York's conception of natural law taps similar anxieties, and the play as a whole depicts a similar process of social disintegration. It is presumably no coincidence that the imagery of bestiality, which begins to gather momentum in this play, rolls with increasing savagery through Part III and *Richard III.*

It is York's doctrine of natural supremacy that welds the Cade revolt securely to the major movement of the play. The rising is both a genuine result of social distress and a political ploy of York's, but it is also a symbolic extension of the anarchy York implicitly sanctions, as his own language suggests. " 'Twas men I lack'd," he muses as he contemplates his journey to Ireland,

> and you will give them me:
> I take it kindly; yet be well assur'd
> You put sharp weapons in a madman's hands.

[15]P. 167.

> Whiles I in Ireland nourish a mighty band
> I will stir up in England some black storm
> Shall blow ten thousand souls to heaven, or hell;
> And this fell tempest shall not cease to rage
> Until the golden circuit on my head,
> Like to the glorious sun's transparent beams,
> Do calm the fury of this mad-bred flaw.
> And, for a minister of my intent,
> I have seduc'd a headstrong Kentishman,
> John Cade of Ashford,
> To make commotion. . . .
>
> [III.i.345-58]

As York proceeds to describe "this stubborn Cade," it becomes increasingly clear that he is depicting not merely a "minister" but a figure who in caricature externalizes his own rebellious lunacy:

> I have seen
> Him caper upright like a wild Morisco,
> Shaking the bloody darts as he his bells.
>
> [III.i.364-66]

When Cade asserts his right to the throne, he mimics, with some help from the Butcher and the Weaver, the very claims of his master, the rights of succession and natural supremacy:

Cade.	My father was a Mortimer,—
But.	[*Aside.*] He was an honest man, and a good bricklayer.
Cade.	My mother a Plantagenet,—
But.	[*Aside.*] I knew her well; she was a midwife.
Cade.	My wife descended of the Lacies,—
But.	[*Aside.*] She was, indeed, a pedlar's daughter, and sold many laces.
Weaver.	[*Aside.*] But not of late, not able to travel with her furr'd pack, she washes bucks here at home.
Cade.	Therefore am I of an honourable house.
But.	[*Aside.*] Ay, by my faith, the field is honourable, and there was he born, under a hedge; for his father had never a house but the cage.
Cade.	Valiant I am.
Weaver.	[*Aside.*] A must needs, for beggary is valiant.
Cade.	I am able to endure much.
But.	[*Aside.*] No question of that, for I have seen him whipp'd three market-days together.
Cade.	I fear neither sword nor fire.

[IV.ii.37-56]

The use of parody in the Cade scenes recalls the treatment of La Pucelle and the French in Part I, though here it performs the subtler function of extension rather than inversion. Cade is neither York's equivalent nor his opposite, but his reductio ad absurdum.

As has been generally observed, the insurrection Shakespeare depicts is actually a conflation of two uprisings, that of Cade and the Peasants' Revolt under Richard II.[16] The report is thus not factually accurate, even by Shakespearean standards. Although several important details are drawn from chronicle accounts of Jack Cade and his followers— the incitement of the Yorkist party, the killing of Lord Say and his brother-in-law, Cade's death at the hands of Alexander Iden—the thematic orientation of the scene derives almost exclusively from the Peasants' Revolt. It is this rising, marked by the communistic preaching of John Ball and the mob's fury against lawyers and the law, that provides the emblematic content of the episode. By fusing the two separate occasions, Shakespeare creates a paradigm of misrule that serves not merely as a tactical consequence of York's decision to seize the throne but as a philosophic extension of all that his attitude toward justice and the law implies.

The Cade revolt thus inverts in grisly comedy the fundamental values of the play. The first request Cade entertains, that of the Butcher, sets the tone for the whole proceedings: "The first thing we do, let's kill all the lawyers" (IV.ii.73). His response is wittily pertinent not only to the Butcher's occupation but, more seriously, to the lingering shadow of the emblematic action with which the good Duke Humphrey greeted Henry's marriage: "Nay, that I mean to do. Is not this a lamentable thing, that of the skin of an innocent lamb should be made parchment? that parchment being scribbled o'er, should undo a man? Some say the bee stings; but I say, 'tis the bee's wax, for I did but seal once to a thing, and I was never mine own man since" (IV.ii.74-79). In a manner typical of the more complex forms of homiletic comedy, Cade's witticisms evoke a peculiarly anxiety-ridden laughter, a merriment that threatens at any moment to turn sour. Indeed, as the insurrection grows increasingly grotesque, laughter gives way increasingly to anxious dread; that it does not vanish altogether is owing to the persistent use of parody, which filters even the most sordid violence through the lenses of literary convention.

Two of the more shocking episodes consist of direct travesties of legal proceedings. Upon entering London, Cade promptly determines that "henceforward it shall be treason for any that calls me other than Lord Mortimer," only to have an unknowing soldier run up shouting "Jack Cade! Jack Cade!" (IV.vi.5-7); he is killed on the spot. The second incident, longer and more grimly pathetic, concerns Lord Say, who as an innocent victim with a firm faith in justice brings to mind once more the dead

---

[16] See Bullough, III, 95-97, 128-33.

Gloucester: "The trust I have is in mine innocence, / And therefore am I bold and resolute" (IV.iv.58-59). The entire Say episode parodies Gloucester's trial, Cade's methods of justice differing from those of Winchester and Suffolk only in the extent of the legal jargon employed: "Ah, thou say, thou serge, nay, thou buckram lord! now art thou within point-blank of our jurisdiction regal. What canst thou answer to my Majesty for giving up of Normandy unto Mounsieur Basimecu, the Dauphin of France? Be it known unto thee by these presence, even the presence of Lord Mortimer, that I am the besom that must sweep the court clean of such filth as thou art" (IV.vii.22-30). The unnatural expertise in foreign affairs recalls the comparable sophistication of the lieutenant who condemns Suffolk, while the specific concern with the loss of the French territories provides yet another link between Cade and York.

The main thrust of the episode is expressed in Cade's "Away! burn all the records of the realm; my mouth shall be the parliament of England." Coupled with John Holland's ominous aside—"Then we are like to have biting statutes, unless his teeth be pull'd out" (IV.vii.12-16)—Cade's rallying cry anticipates the assertion of authority to be made later by York: "Here is a hand to hold a sceptre up, / And with the same to act controlling laws" (V.i.102-3). In the contrast between hand and teeth, it seems, lies the essential difference between the aristocratic and the common rebel.[17] That Cade meets his death in the garden of Iden activates a pun only implicit in the sources:

> Lord! who would live turmoiled in the court,
> And may enjoy such quiet walks as these?
> This small inheritance my father left me
> Contenteth me, and worth a monarchy.
>
> [IV.x.16-19]

The allusion to Eden points up the fallacy of all those who would overturn law in the interest—muddled or shrewd—of returning man to a natural state lost beyond recovery. "The corruption of our nature being presupposed," writes Hooker, "we may not deny but that the Law of Nature doth now require of necessity some kind of regiment; so that to bring things unto the first course they were

---

[17]For an enlightening analysis of the hand imagery used to characterize York, see James L. Calderwood, "Shakespeare's Evolving Imagery: *2 Henry VI*," *English Studies*, 48 (1968), 481-93. "In disputing Henry's right to the crown (V.i.97-98) and in proclaiming his own kingly virtues (V.i.102-3)," Calderwood suggests, "York finds the hand and its functions inordinately relevant. It seems clear that he regards kingship less as a position which imposes responsibilities than as one which licenses power" (p. 492).

in, and utterly to take away all kind of public government in the world, were apparently to overturn the whole world."[18]

The death of Cade brings no restoration of order, since the more dangerous threat of York remains; it is his act of rebellion that concludes the play's exploration of modes of lawlessness and sets the stage for the outright anarchy of Part III. Though York's revolt is in no way condoned, Shakespeare's treatment of its immediate origins casts aspersions on Henry as well. As in Part III, the perspective on all parties is rigorously ironic. York is a rebel, his demand that Somerset be imprisoned a mere ruse. When he discovers that, contrary to Buckingham's oath, Somerset is free, his outburst betrays with fine unconscious irony the hollowness of his position:

> False king! why hast thou broken faith with me,
> Knowing how hardly I can brook abuse?
> King did I call thee? No, thou art not king;
> Not fit to govern and rule multitudes,
> Which dar'st not, no, nor canst not rule a traitor.
>
> [V.i.91-95]

That Henry has "broken faith," however, is indeed true—no matter that York hardly cares. Somerset's awkward arrival on the scene represents on the king's part a political and moral error with disastrous repercussions. That Somerset's appearance before York is tactically inept modern audiences can readily understand; it affords an easy pretext for revolt. Rather more alien is the stress placed on Henry's broken faith. Whether inadvertently or by conscious design, Henry has committed an act that threatens the very basis of all political order: "Since faith is the foundation of justice, which is the chief constitutor and maker of a public weal, and by the aforementioned authority [Aristotle], faith is the conservator of the same, I may therefore conclude that faith is both the original and (as it were) principal constitutor and conservator of the public weal."[19] The betrayal of faith, then, conveys a symbolic significance far greater than the political context of York's revolt suggests. As an act that violates the central values of the play, it is comparable to Henry's thoughtless donning of the red rose in Part I: in the one instance an abuse of ceremony, in the other of justice.[20]

---

[18]*Ecclesiastical Polity*, I, 191.

[19]Elyot, *Governor*, p. 181.

[20]One may argue, as Michael Manheim does, that it is apparently Margaret who is responsible for Somerset's release. But Henry does not even try to order Somerset returned; instead, his reaction is one of uncomfortable complicity: "See, Buckingham,

2 Henry VI ends appropriately, then, with the confusion of the battlefield, lawlessness achieving its apotheosis in civil war. The battle of Saint Albans settles no issues, offers no resolution to the problems established in the play, merely ushers in the conflict that will pervade Part III. New characters emerge—Richard, Edward, Clifford—a new generation that will push the violent propensities of its elders to glorious extremes. Clifford's is the voice that most directly anticipates this brave new world, a voice which on the battlefield sounds curiously reminiscent of an earlier hero:

> He that is truly dedicate to war
> Hath no self-love; nor he that loves himself
> Hath not essentially, but by circumstance,
> The name of valour.
>
> [V.ii.37-40]

There is something of the selflessness of Talbot in this strain, or of Gloucester, yet its perversion is immediate and overwhelming. With the sight of his father's corpse, it is as if Clifford's whole world explodes:

> O! let the vile world end,
> And the premised flames of the last day
> Knit earth and heaven together;
> Now let the general trumpet blow his blast,
> Particularities and petty sounds
> To cease!
>
> [V.ii.40-45]

Caught up in this frenzied vision of doom, Clifford shatters in the name of fatherhood all the communal values invoked by Talbot and Gloucester. Priorities are reversed, hierarchies overturned; community, formerly defined as a chain of loyalties stretching from the individual to God, now extends no farther than the

---

Somerset comes with th'Queen: / Go, bid her hide him quickly from the Duke" (V.i.83-84). Thus, if he does not initiate the act of faithlessness—the text is ambiguous on this point—Henry at least perpetuates it. See *The Weak King Dilemma in the Shakespearean History Play* (Syracuse, N.Y., 1973), p. 102. While he offers a useful corrective to the customary critical contempt of Henry, Manheim is often overzealous in his defense. In praising him as a Christian, Manheim tends to overlook the fact that Henry is to be judged as a Christian king. The distinction is crucial to the play and crucial to humanistic thinking on the nature of kingship throughout the sixteenth century. Erasmus puts it perhaps most succinctly: "It is quite possible to find a good man who would not make a good prince; but there can be no good prince who is not also a good man" (*The Education of a Christian Prince*, tr. L. K. Born [New York, 1936], p. 189).

family circle. In Part I the death scene of the two Talbots anticipates such a shrinkage, but there the primary values of Christian virtue and patriotism reach beyond the family unit. In the case of Clifford, however, family loyalty, cut off from the larger bonds that grant it value and meaning, leads only to hideous perversions:

> Henceforth I will not have to do with pity:
> Meet I an infant of the house of York,
> Into as many gobbets will I cut it
> As wild Medea young Absyrtus did:
> In cruelty will I seek out my fame.
> Come, thou new ruin of old Clifford's house:
> As did Aeneas old Anchises bear,
> So bear I thee upon my manly shoulders;
> But then Aeneas bare a living load,
> Nothing so heavy as these woes of mine.
>
> [V.ii.56-65]

Clifford's exit, as he bears off his father in the manner of Aeneas, recalls with grim irony the action of a hero whose father-love was manifested not in a mindless bloodlust but in piety and service to the state. It is such shrunken and twisted bonds of kinship that sustain the world of Part III.

In the context of the tetralogy as a whole, then, *2 Henry VI* depicts the second stage in a process of social and political decay that begins with the death of Henry V. In Part I the forms of chivalry and ceremony become gradually emptied of all meaning; in Part II the values of justice and the law erode until they collapse in the confusion of civil war. That the conceptual frameworks which sustain these two plays have for Shakespeare a special imaginative power is evident from their recurrence in later works. In Parts I and II of *Henry IV* the concepts of chivalry and justice, while still evocative of social process, are compressed into stages of a single life. In *1 Henry IV* it is the ideal of chivalric heroism that Hal embodies on the battlefield, his virtue played off against the various excesses of Hotspur, "the theme of Honour's tongue" (I.i.81), and Falstaff, for whom "Honour is a mere scutcheon" (V.i.143); we have already observed the ceremonial significance of the "fair rites of tenderness" Hal performs for the dead Percy. In *2 Henry IV* it is justice and the law that serve as the main conceptual frames, appearing in numerous guises—in the figures of the Lord Chief Justice and Justice Shallow, in Prince John's betrayal of the rebels (recall Henry VI's breach of faith), in Hal's climactic rejection of the man who has raced from Gloucestershire to the coronation, singing "the laws of England are at my commandment" (V.iii.134-35).[21]

It goes without saying that the *Henry IV* plays subject these themes to a dramatic and intellectual elaboration far richer than Shakespeare is capable of in *1* and *2 Henry VI*; the mere presence of such correspondences, however, provides evidence of a major line of continuity in the development of Shakespeare's career. Indeed, the vision of social disintegration which so troubles Bolingbroke in *2 Henry IV* but which is forestalled by Hal's emergence as king requires little adaptation to become applicable to the realities of civil war in *3 Henry VI*:

> O my poor kingdom, sick with civil blows!
> When that my care could not withhold thy riots,
> What wilt thou do when riot is thy care?
> O, thou wilt be a wilderness again,
> Peopled with wolves, thy old inhabitants!
>
> [IV.v.134-38]

In the world of the *Henry VI* plays there is unfortunately no Prince Hal, no one to "mock the expectation of the world" or "frustrate prophecies" (V.ii.126-27). In these plays, the process of disintegration seems an inexorable law.

---

[21]John Dover Wilson's argument in *The Fortunes of Falstaff* (Cambridge, 1943) is to the point: "Viewing *Henry IV* as a whole, we may label Part I the Return of Chivalry; Part II the Atonement with Justice" (p. 64). All citations to *2 Henry IV* are from the Arden edition of A. R. Humphreys (London, 1966).

3 *Henry VI:* Kinship

Samuel Johnson probably had *3 Henry VI* in mind when he complained that the *Henry VI* plays "have not sufficient variety of action, for the incidents are too often of the same kind."[1] Of the play's twenty-eight scenes, twelve take place on the battlefield, and the remainder consist for the most part of challenges and counterchallenges, rallying and reassembling of forces—the menacing banalities that serve only to join one bloodbath to the next. A variety of sorts is discernible in all these episodes, even those on the battlefield; there is, after all, more than one way to kill a man—or boy. But the variations are tonal, shades of a dismal gray rather than contrasts of colors. Whether in action or in talk, the mindless violence of civil war pervades the play—a violence stripped bare of chivalric or even rhetorical decorum. It is at the cost of a grisly monotony that the play achieves its distinctive uniformity of tone and its undeniable emotional impact.

The structure of the play is correspondingly indistinct. Unlike Part II, Part III does not move toward a central emotional climax, nor does it embody a unified action. Instead it charts, in a rhythmic series of pulses, the shifting fortunes of Yorkists and Lancastrians from the Battle of Saint Albans to the end of the civil wars. That the vicissitudes of the play's action serve as structural mimicry of the vicissitudes of the wars cataloged by the chroniclers is suggested by Henry's observation on the Battle of Towton:

> Now sways it this way, like a mighty sea
> Forc'd by the tide to combat with the wind;
> Now sways it that way, like the self-same sea
> Forc'd to retire by fury of the wind.
> Sometime the flood prevails, and then the wind;
> Now one the better, then another best;
> Both tugging to be victors, breast to breast;
> Yet neither conqueror nor conquered.
> So is the equal poise of this fell war.
>
> [II.v.5-13][2]

---

[1] *Johnson on Shakespeare*, ed. Arthur Sherbo, Yale Edition of the Works of Samuel Johnson, VIII (New Haven, 1968), 612.
[2] All citations to *3 Henry VI* are from the Arden edition of Andrew S. Cairncross (London, 1964).

The allusions to the natural cycle evoke the interminability of the conflict, a ceaseless flux in which victory and defeat eventually lose all meaning. Even with the final defeat of the Lancastrians at Tewkesbury, distinctions between conqueror and conquered are blurred: Edward sits poised on a throne soon to be undermined by his own brother. The play opens with a Yorkist victory that precipitates years of civil war and ends with one that serves as a prologue to tyranny.

As in Part II, the opening scene of *3 Henry VI* establishes at once the ineffectuality of Henry's rule. His first defeat, on the battlefield, is merely reported—he escaped capture, according to York, because he "slily stole away and left his men" (I.i.3); but his second, in Parliament, is fully dramatized. Confronted by the victorious Yorkists, whose leader has already assumed the throne, Henry displays at first a momentary show of authority:

> Thou factious Duke of York, descend my throne,
> And kneel for grace and mercy at my feet;
> I am thy sovereign.
>
> [I.i.74-76]

But upon York's refusal to budge, the command subsides to a question: "And shall I stand, and thou sit in my throne?" (l. 84); and York remains seated throughout the proceedings. As the scene unfolds, Henry is not merely outfaced but outargued. Having ensnared himself in a specious defense of his title, he confesses in an anxious aside, "I know not what to say: my title's weak" (l. 138). That he succumbs to the pedantic legalism of the Yorkists is typical of Henry's posture throughout the play: if in Part II he is a "providentialist," in Part III he is a weakling and a saint, driven obsessively toward a standard of moral purity at once divine and dangerous to the state. With the sudden appearance of the Yorkist soldiers, Henry simply collapses—outfaced, outargued, outbraved. Grasping at straws, he attempts to salvage his reign by disinheriting his son and relinquishing the crown to York and his heirs. The crisis dissolves finally in the bathos of domestic comedy: confronted with the maternal outrage of his queen, Henry submits passively to her diatribe and acquiesces in her desire for vengeance against the House of York. The unhappy compromise, of course, is promptly and simultaneously broken by both parties.

Abstracted in this manner from the total context of the scene, Henry's ineffectuality seems capable of evoking only bemused contempt from an audience. The actual process of judgment, however, is more complicated. If Henry's weakness is offensive, it is no more so than York's courage. The image of York taunting

3 Henry VI: Kinship

the severed head of Somerset and then proclaiming, with ominous indifference, "By words or blows here let us win our right" (I.i.37) does much to cushion one's criticism of Henry's unrealistic efforts to wage war by "frowns, words, and threats" (l. 72). If Henry's moral sensibility is so refined as to be debilitating, it is only York's coarseness that blinds him to the fact that he is a rebel, not a rightful king—though one must admit that he is not quite so crude as his sons, who urge him to "tear the crown from the usurper's head" (l. 114). Nor is Henry's moral absolutism more objectionable than the oath with which Clifford offers him solace: "King Henry, be thy title right or wrong, / Lord Clifford vows to fight in thy defence . . ." (ll. 163-64). And if Henry is unnatural in disinheriting his son, what is one to say of a wife who overturns at will the political acts of her husband and king?

The perspective throughout the scene, in other words, is unremittingly ironic; here and in the play at large the clash of characters represents a clash of moral positions all of which are fragmentary and imperfect. No longer is there a Talbot or a Gloucester to serve as a center of value, or even a Lucy or an Exeter as chorus. Instead the audience is left to sort out from a world without heroes relative degrees of unworthiness. With the onset of political anarchy, there are simply no heroes left to celebrate and no community to nourish them. And the issues themselves, though clear enough, have become unresolvable. The pressures of the past have exploded in the anarchy of the present, and present actions, as we shall see, spin the future ever farther out of human control. The shift from a mode of drama at least partially eulogistic to one wholly ironic thus marks a natural progression within the movement of the tetralogy as a whole.

Although the issue of political legitimacy figures prominently in the opening scene, it is of little real concern to anyone but Henry, whose moral qualms serve only to unnerve him. But the issue is not solely one of brute force; if it were, there would be nothing to prevent York from seizing Henry and the throne without further ado. Instead, the two claimants, who at this point exercise a restraining influence upon their more aggressive supporters, arrive at a compromise, an accord that lies at the emblematic center of the scene:

K. Hen. . . . . .
                    [*To York*] I here entail
The crown to thee and to thine heirs for ever;
Conditionally that here thou take thine oath
To cease this civil war and, whilst I live,
To honour me as thy king and sovereign;

>   And neither by treason nor hostility
>   To seek to put me down and reign thyself.
> York.   This oath I willingly take and will perform.
>   [*Coming from the throne*]
>
>   [I.i.200-207]

With a sigh of lament at the unnaturalness of his act, Henry disinherits his son that he himself may rule in peace; York forgoes his claim and his seat on the throne that his sons may rule after him. At the core of the scene, then, is a question concerning the nature of parental and filial obligation—a question put to all parties, here and throughout the play, with corrosive irony.

In the opening scene it is Henry's inadequacies that are probed most searchingly. The bond he breaks with a sigh serves as the sole raison d'être for his family and supporters. More familial than political in their loyalties, they recoil with outrage at his act of disinheritance. To Margaret the act violates the most profound ties of nature:

> Ah! wretched man, would I had died a maid,
> And never seen thee, never borne thee son,
> Seeing thou hast prov'd so unnatural a father.
> Hath he deserv'd to lose his birthright thus?
> Hadst thou but lov'd him half so well as I,
> Or felt that pain which I did for him once,
> Or nourish'd him as I did with my blood,
> Thou would'st have left thy dearest heart-blood there,
> Rather than made that savage duke thine heir,
> And disinherited thine only son.
>
>   [I.i.223-32]

Henry has no answer to this, nor to the perceptive query of his son—"If you be king, why should not I succeed?" (l. 234)—but retreats into a timorous acknowledgment that he yielded to the threat of force. Ironically, Henry himself has earlier appealed to the strength of blood-loyalty on two occasions, the first when he rallies his supporters against York:

> Earl of Northumberland, he slew thy father,
> And thine, Lord Clifford; and you both have vow'd revenge
> On him, his sons, his favourites, and his friends.
>
>   [I.i.54-56]

His second appeal enmeshes him in a genealogical argument he would rather avoid. "Are we not both Plantagenets by birth, / And from two brothers lineally descent?" (ll. 125-26), he petitions York, who is only too happy to agree.

3 Henry VI: Kinship

Margaret's accusation of unnaturalness acquires a wealth of ironic significance as her role in the play unfolds, but for the moment it is left to Clifford and the other nobles to betray the insecure foundations of their anger at Henry. For Clifford, Northumberland, and Westmoreland, all of whom have had fathers slain at Saint Albans, the moral and political principles involved in York's claim to the throne are irrelevancies; for them loyalty to Henry ends when he can no longer provide an outlet for the bloodlust of revenge. Clifford's vow to fight for Henry "be thy title right or wrong" is prompted by a filial devotion which already hints at the atrocities that will ensue: "May that ground gape and swallow me alive, / Where I shall kneel to him that slew my father!" (I.i.165-66). And his disgust with Henry's capitulation—"What wrong is this unto the Prince your son!" (l. 182)—wells up from a spirit strangled by the bonds of familial love. To compound the ironies of the situation, Henry himself at one point echoes Clifford's values, threatening that regardless of "right and equity" he will "unpeople" the realm rather than "leave my kingly throne, / Wherein my grandsire and my father sat" (ll. 127-29). While Clifford and Margaret pursue their objectives with the vehemence of narrow minds, Henry merely ties himself in knots of political and moral perplexity.

From Clifford's perspective, as he later makes explicit, York appears an ideal father. Indeed, the fact that he lets slip his own claim to the throne in favor of his sons suggests a devotion to values more generous than that of personal ambition. This compelling paternal love, coupled with the sense of restraint that sets him off from his less inhibited sons, creates a new dimension to the role that York has played thus far in the sequence; in a shift characteristic of the tetralogy's thematic orientation, the "dogged York, that reaches at the moon" (*2 Henry VI* III.i.158) has now become paterfamilias. It is to emphasize this new role that the play begins with York's sons, in a travesty of familial affection (or sibling rivalry), presenting him with gifts of blood. "Richard hath best deserv'd of all my sons" (I.i.17), acknowledges the grateful father as Somerset's head rolls to his feet. York's conception of fatherhood finds expression in acts of violent rebellion and perjury, the latter enabling him to reclaim the throne and to unite once again self-love with family pride.

Family loyalties, then, provide the emblematic core of the opening scene. As a mode of action, a center of value, a measuring rod for the depredations of civil war, kinship, in virtually all its permutations and perversions, serves as the thematic center of the play.³ Among the Lancastrians, the theme is expressed primarily in terms of relations between parent and child, as in the case of Margaret, Henry, and the prince, and in Clifford's obsessive devotion to his dead father. In the Yorkist clan (the word is appropriate), paternal and filial bonds are both at issue, as well as brotherly love. Upon the death of York, Warwick becomes a surrogate father: a shoulder to lean upon (II.i.189); a source of authority—"never will I undertake the thing / Wherein thy counsel and consent is wanting," vows Edward (II.vi.101-2). A host of minor episodes serve as elaborations of these major relationships, variants of the dominant chords. King Lewis responds with exaggerated outrage, for example, at Edward's insult to his daughter; Warwick's daughter seals his compact with Margaret and the prince; the widow Elizabeth captures Edward's hand because she refuses to compromise her honor even for the sake of her children—"thou wrong'st thy children mightily," admonishes Edward, echoing Clifford's appeal to Henry (III.ii.74). Even at the point of Warwick's death his lengthy *de casibus* lament ultimately gives way to a lyrical invocation of his brother Montague, a character whose reported dying words—" 'O farewell, Warwick' " (V.ii.47)—are virtually his first in the play.

As has often been observed, the hint for Shakespeare's exploration of kinship as an index of the horrors of civil war occurs in Hall's account of the Battle of Saxton: "This conflict was in maner unnaturall, for in it the sonne fought against the father, the brother against the brother, the nephew against the uncle, and the tenaunt against his lord...."⁴ The refrain is a familiar one, however, and could just as easily have caught Shakespeare's attention in the final lines of *Gorboduc* or the 1571 *Homily against Disobedience and Wilful Rebellion.* One reason why the *Homily* labels rebellion the "sink and puddle of all sins" is that it disrupts the most intimate of family relations, causing "the brother to seek, and often to work the death of his brother; the son of the father, the father, to seek or procure the death of his sons, being at man's age, and by their faults to disherit their innocent children and kinsmen their heirs for ever, for whom they might purchase livings and lands, as natural parents do take care

---

³Various aspects of this theme are discussed in Don M. Ricks, *Shakespeare's Emergent Form: A Study of the Structures of the* Henry VI *Plays,* Monograph Series, XV, No. 1 (Logan: Utah State University Press, June 1968), pp. 87-95, and Ronald S. Berman, "Fathers and Sons in the *Henry VI* Plays," *Shakespeare Quarterly,* 13 (1962), 494-97.

⁴*Hall's Chronicle* (London, 1809), p. 256.

3 Henry VI: Kinship

and pains, and be at great costs and charges. . . ."[5] What grips the imagination of the moralist is the unnaturalness of such actions. To set Frenchmen and Englishmen at odds is one thing; to set kin against kin is a dreadful violation of the most elemental of all human ties, that of blood. Although Shakespeare may begin with the commonplaces of his sources, he probes far more deeply and extensively, as we have observed in the opening scene, the tragic ironies they embody. In *3 Henry VI*, moreover, the theme of kinship serves not merely to articulate the perversions of civil war but to define a particular stage of historical process. The family is a center of value in the world of *3 Henry VI* because the broader structure of community no longer remains; the social framework has been leveled to its foundations.

It is traditional in Western thought to view the family unit as the bedrock of the state. Cicero's *De Officiis,* a work read by every Elizabethan schoolboy, describes four degrees of social grouping: membership in a common species, a common nation (or language), a common city, a common family. Since the bond of alliance tightens as the social units decrease in size, the family constitutes the most natural and indissoluble of communities, "the original of a citie and as it were the seedplotte of a commonweale."[6] Although the strongest and most elemental of bonds, kinship is for Cicero not the most perfect. Above it in his hierarchy of values is true friendship, based on moral and spiritual affinity rather than ties of blood; and higher still is patriotism, a love which spurs Cicero to castigate the "beastly cruelty" of those people who "have rent a sonder their countrey with al maner of mischief. . . ."[7] In centering *3 Henry VI* on the concept of the family, then, Shakespeare adapts a traditional conception of social structure to the theme of social devolution begun in Part I: chivalric community gives way to the narrower bonds of law, law to kinship, and kinship, as we shall see, to self-love.

That ties of blood should be less sacred than spiritual affinity is made painfully clear by the depredations of the two chief spokesmen for "natural" affection in Scene i, Clifford and Margaret. Clifford's father-love, which began in Part II as a travesty of the piety of Aeneas, assumes in Part III maniacal proportions. With words that betray his stifled humanity, he cuts

---

[5] *Certain Sermons or Homilies Appointed to Be Read in the Churches in the Time of Queen Elizabeth* (Philadelphia, 1844), p. 511.
[6] *Thre Bokes of Duties,* tr. N. Grimald (London, 1556), C6.
[7] *Duties,* C7.

off the pleas of the defenseless young Rutland whom he meets at Wakefield: "In vain thou speak'st, poor boy; my father's blood / Hath stopp'd the passage where thy words should enter" (I.iii.21-22). The startling jolt of sympathy in the phrase "poor boy" and the evasion of personal responsibility for his deafness are telling reminders of an idealism permanently crippled on the field at Saint Albans. For Clifford, filial love ultimately reduces all of life to a terrible geometric simplicity. In a phrase and a deed, he crystallizes the revenge-ethic that dominates the play in a variety of guises: "Thy father slew my father; therefore die. [*Stabs him*]" (l. 46). The "natural" affection that drives Margaret to protect her child's right to the throne finds outlets even more brutal and perverse. Unlike Clifford, who at least hints at suppressed compassion, Margaret inflicts upon her enemy the most insidious of torments:

> Look, York: I stain'd this napkin with the blood
> That valiant Clifford with his rapier's point
> Made issue from the bosom of the boy;
> And if thine eyes can water for his death,
> I give thee this to dry thy cheeks withal.
>
> [I.iv.79-83]

In his treatment of Clifford and Margaret and the play's other avengers, Shakespeare depends upon the standard formulas of the revenge play; in placing these conventions within the framework of civil war and the historical process out of which it emerges, however, he shapes them to new and dramatically compelling ends.

Prompted by Holinshed's allusion to the taunting of Christ by the Jews, J. P. Brockbank remarks on the overtones of the Passion in the scene of York's death.[8] Although present, such resonances are subdued; more important is the narrower, more intense range of associations evoked by the twin emblems of York's suffering, the paper crown and the bloody napkin. In these two symbols are compressed the dominant motives of his life—political aspiration and paternal love. Although both serve as targets for Margaret's derision, it is York's love of his son that generates the greatest force, transforming his Passion into an unholy martyrdom to the great god of fatherhood. It is the blood of young Rutland, not the paper crown, that drives York to an emotional climax so eloquent that it moves even Northumberland to tears:

---

[8]"The Frame of Disorder: *Henry VI*," in *Early Shakespeare* (Stratford-upon-Avon Studies 3), ed. John Russell Brown and Bernard Harris (New York, 1961), p. 95.

> That face of his the hungry cannibals
> Would not have touch'd, would not have stain'd with blood;
> But you are more inhuman, more inexorable—
> O, ten times more—than tigers of Hyrcania.
> See, ruthless queen, a hapless father's tears.
> This cloth thou dipp'd'st in blood of my sweet boy,
> And I with tears do wash the blood away.
> Keep thou the napkin, and go boast of this;
> And if thou tell the heavy story right,
> Upon my soul, the hearers will shed tears;
> Yea, even my foes will shed fast-falling tears;
> And say "Alas! it was a piteous deed."
>
> [I.iv.152-63]

When one casts a backward glance at the course of York's career, a grim but fitting irony can be seen in the manner of his death, subjected as he is to a humiliating travesty of the very ideals he himself has perverted. Indeed, even his hope for vengeance recoils against him with a prophetic irony of which he is unaware: "My ashes, like the phoenix, may bring forth / A bird that will revenge upon you all ..." (ll. 35-36). Yet the perception of these ironies merely brings home the extent to which Shakespeare subordinates them to the sheer intensity of human grief and thus transcends the narrow moral didacticism of his sources. One is reminded of a later scene in which ironic moral judgments are dissipated by a character's suffering, that of Gloucester's blinding in *King Lear*.

The atrocities committed by Clifford and Margaret in the name of family loyalty create a new perspective on their ensuing relations with Henry, especially at their next encounter, when Henry's refusal to gloat at the sight of York's head as it sits on the gates of his town prompts a rebuke from Clifford for "too much lenity" and a lecture taken from the book of nature:

> Unreasonable creatures feed their young;
> And though man's face be fearful to their eyes,
> Yet, in protection of their tender ones,
> Who hath not seen them, even with those wings
> Which sometime they have us'd with fearful flight,
> Make war with him that climb'd unto their nest,
> Offering their own lives in their young's defence?
> For shame, my liege, make them your precedent!
>
> [II.ii.26-33]

We have already observed where this line of argument leads, what kind of precedents Margaret and Clifford have drawn from the behavior of "unreasonable" creatures. One wonders whether Henry is so "unnatural" a father. In appealing to natural instinct, Clifford activates a concept fraught with serious ambiguities:

"between man, and beaste, this chiefly is the difference," writes Cicero in the *Offices,* "that a beaste, so far as he is moved by sense, bendeth himself to that onely, which is present, and at hand: verie smallie perceiving ought past, or tocome...."[9] The very examples Clifford cites elsewhere in his speech, in fact, allude directly to the various outrages committed thus far in the name of natural feeling. As he urges Henry to act the lion (l. 11) or the bear (l. 13) or the serpent (l. 15), one recalls earlier images: of Clifford himself—"So looks the pent-up lion o'er the wretch / That trembles under his devouring paws..." (I.iii.12-13); of York—"as a bear, encompass'd round with dogs" (II.i.15); of Margaret—"She-wolf of France, but worse than wolves of France, / Whose tongue more poisons than the adder's tooth!" (I.iv.111-12). York's "O tiger's heart wrapp'd in a woman's hide!" (I.iv.137) serves as an emblem for all those characters who, like Clifford, confuse naturalness with bestiality.

As much as one recoils against Clifford's advice in this scene, Henry's rebuttal offers no alternative:

> Full well hath Clifford play'd the orator,
> Inferring arguments of mighty force.
> But, Clifford, tell me, didst thou never hear
> That things evil got had ever bad success?
> And happy always was it for that son
> Whose father for his hoarding went to hell?
> I'll leave my son my virtuous deeds behind;
> And would my father had left me no more!
>
> [II.ii.43-50]

The ironies in the exchange are finely honed, Henry turning with well-placed sarcasm from Clifford's book of nature to his own stock of proverbial lore. "The general and perpetual voice of men," writes Hooker, "is as the sentence of God himself."[10] Although a shrewd rejoinder to Clifford's harangue, Henry's response is not, as Ronald S. Berman suggests, an "intensely noble expression."[11] The king who directs his kneeling prince to "draw thy sword in right" (l. 62) suffers from a moral paralysis that prevents him from drawing his sword at all. Both characters elevate half-truths to the level of absolutes. Only the young prince's attitude seems appropriate to the situation, combining respect for authority with a firm resolve to retain his rights:

---

[9] *Duties*, A5^v.
[10] *Of the Laws of Ecclesiastical Polity* (London, 1907), I, 176.
[11] Berman, p. 496.

3 Henry VI: Kinship

> My gracious father, by your kingly leave,
> I'll draw it [the sword] as apparent to the crown,
> And in that quarrel use it to the death.
>
> [II.ii.63-65]

Though his role is underplayed, Prince Edward consistently strikes the necessary balance between Henry's "too much lenity"—what Elyot in *The Governor* calls "vain pity"[12]—and Clifford's cruelty. The scene's dialectical technique, though not fully realized, clearly foreshadows that of the *Henry IV* plays. The implications of the prince's response, moreover—that true legitimacy is not inherited but earned—are pursued not only in the figure of Prince Hal but in the Bastard Falconbridge in *King John*.

The dialogue between Clifford and Henry continues obliquely in a series of scenes juxtaposed with sharply ironic effect. In Act II Scene iv Richard and Clifford, alone in the midst of battle, exchange furious taunts and blows until Warwick enters and Clifford is forced to flee. In Act II Scene v Henry, alone on a molehill, yearns for the pastoral life until his thoughts are interrupted by the entrance of the father who has killed his son and the son who has killed his father; Henry too finally exits fleeing. In Act II Scene vi Clifford, with an arrow in his neck, levies his final judgment on Henry and dies. His corpse is taunted by the encircling Yorkists, who now have a head to take the place of York's on the gates of the city. In the next scene, Act III Scene i, Henry himself is captured by the foresters as he steals home from Scotland, disguised, and with a prayer book in hand.

The vicious exchange between Clifford and Richard sets the stage for the most important scene in the series, that of Henry's pastoral lament (II.v). In its inconsequential relation to the outcome of the plot and its stylized, emblematic manner, the "mole-hill" scene resembles the Countess of Auvergne episode in Part I and the "miracle" of Saint Albans in Part II; more than either of these earlier episodes, it generates a complicated response. The scene begins with Henry, alone, musing upon the vicissitudes of the battle that swirls around him; as he sits upon a molehill, his thoughts turn to the simplicity and order of a shepherd's life:

> O God! methinks it were a happy life
> To be no better than a homely swain;
> To sit upon a hill, as I do now,
> To carve out dials quaintly, point by point,

---

[12] See *The Governor*, ed. S. E. Lehmberg (London, 1962), pp. 115-20.

> Thereby to see the minutes how they run—
> How many makes the hour full complete,
> How many hours brings about the day,
> How many days will finish up the year,
> How many years a mortal man may live.
> When this is known, then to divide the times—
> So many hours must I tend my flock;
> So many hours must I take my rest;
> So many hours must I contemplate;
> So many hours must I sport myself;
> So many days my ewes have been with young;
> So many weeks ere the poor fools will ean;
> So many years ere I shall shear the fleece:
> So minutes, hours, days, weeks, months, and years,
> Pass'd over to the end they were created,
> Would bring white hairs unto a quiet grave.
> Ah, what a life were this! how sweet! how lovely!
> [II.v.21-41]

Remarking upon the manner in which the lines of Henry's "exquisite pastoral seem to re-create the convention out of the kind of human experience which underlies it," J. P. Brockbank calls the soliloquy "the most moving of Shakespeare's comments on the civil wars."[13]

That Henry's yearning for a pastoral life affords a moment of sanity in welcome contrast to the chaos of civil war is certainly true. Coming as it does immediately after the savage encounter between Clifford and Richard on the battlefield—not to mention the earlier atrocities—Henry's longing to isolate himself from such madness cannot help but touch a responsive chord. Yet the effect of the speech, given the total dramatic context, is double edged. If on the one hand Henry's idyll provides a release from the brutality of the battlefield, on the other it presents no solution to the conflict. The war rages, after all, in part because of the very instincts toward retreat that Henry is at this point once more indulging; the Lancastrians are even now without a leader. Contemplated from this angle, the detached passivity of Henry's pose becomes ironic. The pastoral vision implies a comment on the civil wars, as Brockbank maintains, but it also implies a comment on the nature of Henry's rule.

The pastoral conventions upon which the scene depends, moreover, provide their own implicit commentary. To compare a king's life to that of a shepherd is to invoke automatically one of the political commonplaces of the period. In More's *Utopia*, for

[13]P. 96.

3 Henry VI: Kinship

example, Hythlodaeus describes the duties of kingship in terms that were familiar to most educated Elizabethans: "Suppose I should show that they [the people] choose a king for their own sake and not for his—to be plain, that by his labor and effort they may live well and safe from injustice and wrong. For this very reason, it belongs to the king to take more care for the welfare of his people than for his own, just as it is the duty of a shepherd, insofar as he is a shepherd, to feed his sheep rather than himself."[14] The very language of his lament thus suggests the extent to which Henry's desire to become a shepherd represents an evasion of his responsibilities as king. The mood created by the episode as a whole is one of pathos mingled with irony.

The pastoral motif reappears as late as *Henry V* in a moment of personal crisis, in the king's soliloquy the night before Agincourt, though this time in a version so realistic and so tightly compressed as to be scarcely recognizable. Henry V's envy is directed not at a shepherd but at a peasant, the "wretched slave" who,

> like a lackey, from the rise to set
> Sweats in the eye of Phoebus, and all night
> Sleeps in Elysium; next day after dawn,
> Doth rise and help Hyperion to his horse,
> And follows so the ever-running year
> With profitable labour to his grave. . . .
> [IV.i.278-83]

The classical allusions betray the potentially dangerous idealization of apolitical experience inherent in such sentiments—an idealization that Henry V, unlike his son, is able to overcome.

As Henry VI's idyll yields to the successive lamentations of the father and son, the overtones of tragic responsibility resonate with even greater urgency. An emblem of the war itself interrupts the pastoral dream. "O pity, pity, gentle heaven, pity!" pleads Henry as he observes the grief-stricken father:

> The red rose and the white are on his face,
> The fatal colours of our striving houses:
> The one his purple blood right well resembles;
> The other his pale cheeks, methinks, presenteth.
> Wither one rose, and let the other flourish!
> If you contend, a thousand lives must wither.
> [II.v.96-102]

---

[14]*Utopia*, ed. Edward Surtz, S.J. (New Haven, 1964), pp. 45-46. As Surtz observes, the motif "occurs everywhere"; he cites, among others, Ezek. 34:2, Jer. 23:1; Hom. *Il*. 2.243, 4.296; Pl. *Rep*. 1.345; Arist. *Eth. Nic*. 8.11.1, 1161a.

As king and commoners join in choric lament, a new topos emerges to place Henry's grief once more in the widest possible context:

Son.	How will my mother for a father's death
	Take on with me and ne'er be satisfied!
Fath.	How will my wife for slaughter of my son
	Shed seas of tears and ne'er be satisfied!
K. Hen.	How will the country for these woeful chances
	Misthink the King and not be satisfied!
Son.	Was ever son so rued a father's death?
Fath.	Was ever father so bemoan'd his son?
K. Hen.	Was ever king so griev'd for subjects' woe?
	Much is your sorrow; mine, ten times so much.

[II.v.103-12]

No longer shepherd of his country, Henry is now its father, his sorrow magnified in proportion to his loss. That Henry feels with great intensity the human significance of the civil wars sets him apart from the savagery around him; like his yearning for pastoral tranquility, his generalized grief vents emotions by this time sorely in need of expression. Yet here too the topos turns ironically against him; the father and son are victims of a situation which Henry's ineffectuality has helped bring into being. That York suffered earlier on the same molehill calls attention to the parallel in their fates as fathers; York's ambition results in his own and Rutland's death, Henry's passivity in the suffering of his land. Unlike York's grief, however, which ultimately dissipates all ironies, Henry's lamentations are contained within a firmly ironic perspective. The scene's final image is of Henry fleeing:

> Nay, take me with thee, good sweet Exeter:
> Not that I fear to stay, but love to go
> Whither the Queen intends. Forward; away!

[II.v.137-39]

Not until his own death, paradoxically, does Henry face life like a king.

As Henry races offstage, Clifford staggers on, an arrow in his neck. With his dying words he foresees the king's defeat and inveighs against the weakness that has brought tragedy to the realm:

> Oh, Lancaster, I fear thy overthrow
> More than my body's parting with my soul.
> My love and fear glu'd many friends to thee;
> And, now I fall, thy tough commixture melts,
> Impairing Henry, strengthening misproud York.
> . . . . .

3 Henry VI: Kinship

> And, Henry, hadst thou sway'd as kings should do,
> Or as thy father, and his father did,
> Giving no ground unto the house of York,
> They never then had sprung like summer flies;
> I, and ten thousand in this luckless realm
> Had left no mourning widows for our death;
> And thou this day hadst kept thy chair in peace.
> For what doth cherish weeds but gentle air?
> And what makes robbers bold but too much lenity?
> [II.vi.3-7,14-22]

In its combination of prophetic insight and homiletic urgency the speech recalls the choric commentaries of Lucy and Exeter in Part I. The charge of "too much lenity," indeed, repeats a phrase used earlier by Clifford in his argument with Henry (II.ii.9), while the image of ten thousand mourning widows reflects immediately upon the lamentations of the preceding scene. Unlike Lucy and Exeter, however, Clifford is no faceless authorial spokesman but a fully individualized character—a man who in his final moments of life remains too morally obtuse to comprehend the irony in his accusations. The blend of conventional didactic commentary with a psychological verisimilitude that partially undermines it adds a new dimension to Shakespeare's handling of the soliloquy. A further stage occurs in *Richard III*, when irony moves into the character's own psyche and commentary becomes self-conscious.

As Clifford himself intimates, his passing prefigures the emergence of a new order; with his death and York's the ideal of family loyalty gradually crumbles. It lingers on in Clarence's spontaneous reunion with his brothers at Coventry and, most powerfully, in Margaret's torment at the murder of the prince, but by then such gestures are no more than the afterglow of values long extinguished. The first hint of the dissolution of the tight-knit Yorkist clan occurs early in the play, in the wondrous vision of the three suns that seem so clearly a symbol of brotherly unity. Richard's description of the merging of the three into one image, however, conveys with prophetic ambiguity a hint of the actual future, in which dissembled affection enables him to absorb his brothers and shine alone:

> See, see! they join, embrace, and seem to kiss,
> As if they vow'd some league inviolable:
> Now are they but one lamp, one light, one sun.
> [II.i.29-31]

After the temporary dislocation of Clarence's defection, this unity is celebrated in the family gathering that closes the play, highlighted by Richard's Judas kiss.

With the ascendancy of Edward, the Yorkist brotherhood proves incapable of surviving the strains of power. The immediate cause of their disaffection, and that of the surrogate father Warwick, is Edward's lust. Unable to bed the Lady Elizabeth on his own terms, Edward lurches into an ignoble and impolitic marriage, and then proceeds to elevate his wife's kinsmen at the expense of his own brothers. Though significantly less idealized than Henry's, Edward's infatuation echoes in its disastrous consequences the passion of the former king for Margaret in Part I. Unmoved by the protests of Clarence and Richard, the new ruler seals in a phrase his devotion to brotherhood, friendship, and the welfare of the realm at large: "I am Edward, / Your King and Warwick's, and must have my will" (IV.i.15-16). So much for the selflessness of family loyalty. One recalls Cade, whose mouth was to become the parliament of England; York's progeny themselves now emerge as parodies of their father. Edward's willfulness proves immediately self-destructive, of course, shattering his relations with his brothers, Warwick, and France, and making possible a new alliance between his enemies and former friends.

Although the defections of Clarence and Warwick create new turmoil among both parties, their self-assertiveness is inconsequential when compared to Richard's. From the moment of his first soliloquy (III.ii), Richard usurps a position of prominence he retains until the aftermath of Bosworth Field. From the perspective of character development, Richard's sudden emergence as a self-conscious violator of all bonds of family affection seems somewhat disconcerting. For the first half of the play, though distinguished from Edward by his fiery nature in war and his sophistry in peace, Richard betrays none of the vicious alienation characteristic of his later self-revelations. Indeed, in keeping with the thematic emphasis on familial devotion, Richard is shown time and again expressing without irony the appropriate emotions, whether at his father's death—"Richard, I bear thy name; I'll venge thy death, / Or die renowned by attempting it" (II.i.87-88); or on the battlefield with Edward and Warwick:

> Brother, give me thy hand; and, gentle Warwick,
> Let me embrace thee in my weary arms:
> I, that did never weep, now melt with woe
> That winter should cut off our spring-time so.
>
> [II.iii.44-47]

A psychological approach to Richard's sudden shift in character, though plausible in some respects, can only yield ambiguous results. M. M. Reese, for example, suggests that in soliloquy

Richard "reveals himself as the solitary hunter that at heart he has always been"; Robert Ornstein, on the other hand, finds in the death of York a "spiritual turning point" that leaves Richard "without a single emotional attachment."[15]

It is futile to choose between such opposed interpretations; like Clifford's, Richard's sudden dominance as a character is motivated by only shadowy outlines of psychological development. The stages of Richard's "development," like those of other characters—Henry's, say, or York's—are defined with less attention to the inner workings of individual psychology than to the general vision of social and historical process that unifies the tetralogy. As loyalty to the family dissolves, a new and ominous individualism emerges to take its place. The suggestion for Richard's sudden dominance seems to have come from a general observation in More's *Richard III*, not from psychological intuition. "No where," laments the dying Edward to his factious kinsmen, "finde we so dedly debate as emongst theim whiche by nature and lawe moste ought to agre together. Suche a serpente is ambicion and desire of vainglory and sovereigntie, which emongest estates when he is once entred he crepith furth so far, till with devision and variaunce he turneth all to mischiefe."[16] It is this serpent ambition that triggers Richard's soliloquy:

> Ay, Edward will use women honourably.
> Would he were wasted, marrow, bones, and all,
> That from his loins no hopeful branch may spring,
> To cross me from the golden time I look for!
>
> [III.ii.124-27]

In modulating from family love to self-assertion at midpoint in the play, then, Shakespeare incorporates a traditional conception of family dynamics into the larger process of social disintegration.

Despite Shakespeare's subordination of psychological to thematic development, the lines just quoted are enough to show the acuteness of his psychological insight. Edward's marriage poses a double menace to Richard, expressed with great psychological subtlety in the very terms of his protest; the "loins" of his brother are threatening to Richard not only because he is ambitious but because he is deformed. Shakespeare's exploration of the psychological impact of Richard's deformity, which begins at this point, constitutes his most significant contribution to the character portrayed in the historical sources. For Thomas More,

---

[15] *The Cease of Majesty* (New York, 1961), p. 204; *A Kingdom for a Stage* (Cambridge, Mass., 1972), p. 58.

the mere fact of ambition is motive enough; the biblical image of the "serpent," in fact, suggests that psychologizing in such a case would be merely redundant. In More's history Richard's abnormal birth becomes a probable sign "that nature chaunged his course in his beginnynge, whiche in his life many thynges unnaturally committed...."[17] Although Shakespeare incorporates this platonic strain into his portrait of Richard—both Henry and, in *Richard III*, Margaret emblematize the deformity—the soliloquies reflect a more modern, Baconian orientation. "It is good to consider of deformity," writes Bacon, "not as a sign, which is more deceivable; but as a cause, which seldom faileth of the effect. Whosoever hath any thing fixed in his person that doth induce contempt, hath also a perpetual spur in himself to rescue and deliver himself from scorn."[18] A comparable intuition underlies Richard's "Love forswore me in my mother's womb" (III.ii.153). The modernity of this viewpoint should not be exaggerated, however, for both Shakespeare and Bacon resist the deterministic implications of their thought. When Richard chooses to break out of his "thorny wood" with a "bloody axe" (l. 181), he does so by an act of will; in Bacon's words, "there is in man an election touching the frame of his mind," though there may be "a necessity in the frame of his body."[19]

Even in Richard's deformity, however, there is more than psychology at work. His description of his birth, while psychologically compelling in its self-abhorrence, has ramifications that extend well beyond the confines of a single mind:

> Why, Love forswore me in my mother's womb:
> And, for I should not deal in her soft laws,
> She did corrupt frail Nature with some bribe,
> To shrink mine arm up like a wither'd shrub;
> To make an envious mountain on my back,
> Where sits Deformity to mock my body;
> To shape my legs of an unequal size;
> To disproportion me in every part,
> Like to a chaos, or unlick'd bear-whelp
> That carries no impression like the dam.
>
> [III.ii.153-62]

---

[16]*Hall's Chronicle*, p. 344. I quote from Hall's adaptation of More's *Richard III*, since Shakespeare apparently had no access to the original.

[17]Ibid., p. 343.

[18]"Of Deformity," *The Works of Francis Bacon*, ed. James Spedding, R. L. Ellis, and D. D. Heath, VI (London, 1890), 480.

[19]Ibid.

3 *Henry VI*: Kinship

The imagery of disordered nature swells Richard's deformity into an emblem of a disordered world, a world unnatural, disproportioned, formless. It is in one sense time itself that has given birth to Richard, the chaos of civil war breeding the "unlick'd bear-whelp" whose only future is savage destruction. With the catalog of villainous devices that concludes the soliloquy, moreover, Richard recapitulates not only the wiles of his father but the accumulated arts of all the "politicians" of Parts I and II:

> Why, I can smile, and murder whiles I smile,
> And cry "Content!" to that that grieves my heart,
> And wet my cheeks with artificial tears,
> And frame my face to all occasions.
>
> [III.ii.182-85]

Henceforth he will dominate the world as a true distillation of the anarchic tendencies of the society that brought him into being.

When Richard confronts Henry in the Tower, the polarities extend from the demonic to the divine. No longer ensnared in the coils of kingship, Henry's saintliness is redeemed by his irrelevance to earthly affairs. The ironic detachment that surfaced earlier in his thrusts against Clifford has now become sharper and more finely tuned. Unlike Richard II, Henry inflicts no physical pain on his tormentor, but the barbs of his sainted wit cut deep:

> K. Hen. . . . . .
> But wherefore dost thou come? Is't for my life?
> Rich. Think'st thou I am an executioner?
> K. Hen. A persecutor I am sure thou art:
> If murdering innocents be executing,
> Why then thou art an executioner.
> Rich. Thy son I kill'd for his presumption.
> K. Hen. Hadst thou been kill'd when first thou didst presume,
> Thou hadst not liv'd to kill a son of mine.
>
> [V.vi.29-36]

With the prophetic insight displayed earlier in his blessing of the young Richmond, Henry foresees his country's future and seals his own doom:

> K. Hen. . . . . .
> Teeth hadst thou in thy head when thou wast born,
> To signify thou cam'st to bite the world;
> And if the rest be true which I have heard,
> Thou cam'st—
> Rich. I'll hear no more: die, prophet, in thy speech. *Stabs him.*
> For this, amongst the rest, was I ordain'd.
> K. Hen. Ay, and for much more slaughter after this.
> O God, forgive my sins and pardon thee! *Dies.*
>
> [V.vi.53-60]

At the moment of his murder, the saintliness that afflicts Henry throughout the play achieves an apotheosis untainted by irony.

In the act of regicide Richard drives the moral anarchy of his peers and predecessors to overtly demonic extremes. Not only does he murder a defenseless king, but he subjects the prostrate corpse to a gratuitous second thrust: "If any spark of life be yet remaining, / Down, down to hell; and say I sent thee thither— [*Stabs him again*]" (V.vi.66-67). Although Richard's brutality transcends even that of Clifford or Margaret, especially in its insinuations of diabolic agency, it adds merely a new variation to a pattern of violence already well established. Not his action but his articulation of motives propels Richard outside the moral framework of the play:

> The midwife wonder'd, and the women cried
> "O jesu bless us, he is born with teeth!"
> And so I was, which plainly signified
> That I should snarl, and bite, and play the dog.
> Then, since the heavens have shap'd my body so,
> Let hell make crook'd my mind to answer it.
> I have no brother, I am like no brother;
> And this word "love", which greybeards call divine,
> Be resident in men like one another,
> And not in me: I am myself alone.
>
> [V.vi.74-83]

The stress on love reflects, no doubt, Shakespeare's reading of the sources in preparation for *Richard III*. In More's history Edward IV invokes the doctrine of charity when he makes the speech of reconciliation that resonates throughout the narrative: "wherefore in these laste woordes that ever I looke to speake to you, I exhorte and require you all, for the love that you have borne too me, and for the love that I have borne to you, and for the love that oure Lorde beareth to us all: From this tyme forward all greves forgotten, eche of you love other...."[20] In *3 Henry VI* Richard's violation of charity is assimilated into the broader vision of social dissolution characteristic of the tetralogy as a whole. In repudiating family ties Richard casts off self-consciously the only social ideal remaining in a world shattered by civil war; in repudiating all love, he cuts himself off from the wider network of values symbolized earlier in Talbot's devotion to chivalry or Gloucester's to law. Both visually and verbally Richard cannot help but bring to mind the earlier hero, Talbot. It was Talbot, after all, whom the Countess of Auvergne mocked as a "weak and writhled shrimp"

---

[20] *Hall's Chronicle*, p. 345.

3 Henry VI: Kinship

(*1 Henry VI* II.iii.22), and Talbot too whose nature was defined in terms of an allegiance to a community ordered by bonds of love: "I am but shadow of myself" (l. 51). Richard's "I am myself alone" thus captures in an aphorism of self-definition the final result of the social disintegration traced throughout the sequence as a whole.

Part III of *Henry VI*, then, depicts the gradual dissolution of a society at war with itself, a society in which the single bond of kinship, isolated from the higher values that must sustain it, becomes increasingly corrupted and is finally destroyed. The vision of social anarchy portrayed in the play lingers on in Shakespeare's imagination throughout his career. Ulysses' famous speech on degree in *Troilus and Cressida* evokes images of a disordered world reminiscent of that depicted in *3 Henry VI*:

> Take but degree away, untune that string,
> And hark what discord follows! Each thing meets
> In mere oppugnancy: the bounded waters
> Should lift their bosoms higher than the shores
> And make a sop of all this solid globe;
> Strength should be lord of imbecility,
> And the rude son should strike his father dead;
> Force should be right; or, rather, right and wrong—
> Between whose endless jar justice resides—
> Should lose their names, and so should justice too.
> Then everything includes itself in power,
> Power into will, will into appetite;
> And appetite, an universal wolf,
> So doubly seconded with will and power,
> Must make perforce an universal prey,
> And last eat up himself. Great Agamemnon,
> This chaos, when degree is suffocate,
> Follows the choking.
>
> [I.iii.109-26]

Within the context of *Troilus and Cressida* Ulysses' pronouncement is subject to an ironic perspective that mocks its apparent profundity; his rhetoric, like that of others, is hopelessly divorced from effective action. The emphasis on degree, moreover, creates a more limited conceptual framework than that established throughout the *Henry VI* plays. But the powerful vision of disrupted family bonds, of the mindless lust for power, of moral and social chaos has its origins, it seems, in the world of *3 Henry VI*. In retrospect, moreover, the image of the wolf that ultimately devours himself gives added poignance to the play's many allusions to bestiality and to the stress on cannibalism that accentuates the brutality of its final moments.[21] While Margaret curses the murderers of her son—"Butchers and villains! bloody cannibals!" (V.v.59)—Richard is on his way to a "bloody supper in the Tower" (l. 83). In *Richard III*, as we shall see, Richard takes special pleasure in dining after executions and marks the beginning of his downfall by gnawing his lip. The concluding play of the tetralogy thus carries on the process of social dissolution embodied in Ulysses' speech into its final, apocalyptic phase, when Richard III, a universal wolf, devours the world around him and, finally, himself.

[21] For a discussion of the imagery of bestiality, see Berman, p. 497.

Richard III: The Self Alone

Unlike the *Henry VI* plays, *Richard III* has not suffered the general indifference of critics and scholars; its position as the first of Shakespeare's undoubted artistic triumphs has attracted a great deal of sympathetic criticism. For literary historians the play has been of especial interest as a complex assimilation of a wide variety of dramatic and literary traditions—among them, Senecan drama, *de casibus* tragedy, the Vice-figure of the morality plays, and the historical narrative of Thomas More.[1] For most recent critics the chief concern has been the unity of the play itself—its elaborate symmetries ranging from Senecan stichomythia in the dialogue to broad structural patterns, its unremitting focus on the nature and fortunes of a single hero.[2] Of the many interpretations of *Richard III,* however, few have assessed its relationship to the *Henry VI* plays. In part the lack of concern for such a perspective can be attributed to Tillyard's failure to establish its usefulness.[3] In part, too, it can be attributed to the play's obvious unity, which insures a self-sufficiency denied to any other play in the series. Yet the neglect of the *Henry VI* plays has been partially responsible for some severe distortions of the significance of *Richard III.* The distinctive features of the titular hero and the play's conception of historical process derive from literary dynamics more personal than the influences of Seneca or More or the morality tradition, dynamics set in motion by the *Henry VI* plays themselves.

As the conclusion to a series of plays in which characterization is rarely complex (by Shakespearean standards) and is customarily subordinated to theme, Shakespeare creates in *Richard III* a play with a protagonist of such dimensions as to have attracted the

---

[1] See especially Wolfgang Clemen, *A Commentary of Shakespeare's* Richard III, tr. Jean Bonheim (London, 1968); Bernard Spivack, *Shakespeare and the Allegory of Evil* (New York, 1958), pp. 386-407; Virgil K. Whitaker, *Shakespeare's Use of Learning* (San Marino, Calif., 1953), pp. 45-81.

[2] See particularly Nicholas Brooke, *Shakespeare's Early Tragedies* (London, 1968), pp. 48-79, and A. P. Rossiter, "Angel with Horns: The Unity of *Richard III,*" in *Angel with Horns and Other Shakespearean Lectures* (London, 1961), pp. 1-22.

[3] E. M. W. Tillyard, *Shakespeare's History Plays* (London, 1944), pp. 227-45. For a terse but effective critique of Tillyard's approach, see John Dover Wilson's introduction to the 1954 Cambridge edition, pp. xliii-xiv.

greatest actors from the eighteenth century to the present—Garrick, Kean, Macready, Irving, and, most recently, Olivier.[4] One can explain this curious shift in dramatic mode, of course, as the result of Marlovian or Senecan influences or the imaginative impact of the characterization by More (Richard was a bogeyman before Shakespeare took him over). But its motivation lies closer to home, in Richard's emergence at the end of *3 Henry VI* as the final product of the anarchic tendencies of civil dissension and cival war. *3 Henry VI* concludes, as we have seen, with a gigantic assertion of the dominance of the self: "I am myself alone" (V.vi.83). *Richard III* opens with stage directions embodying dramatically that impulse: "*Enter Richard, Duke of Gloucester, solus*"; and the remainder of the play explores the nature of this self alone as he moves from conquest to destruction. It is thus through "the eminence of Richard's character," not in spite of it, as Tillyard contends, that Shakespeare brings to completion the national tetralogy.[5]

It is typical of the assimilative manner of the play that Richard's opening soliloquy blends an acute psychological realism with the allegorical conventions of the Vice. As Bernard Spivack has shown, it is the Vice tradition that, throughout the first half of the play, at least, accounts for the role's peculiar mixture of sardonic wit and deceitful aggression and, above all, its seductive intimacy with the audience.[6] But coupled to this role is a more modern, psychological one:

> Why, I, in this weak piping time of peace,
> Have no delight to pass away the time,
> Unless to spy my shadow in the sun
> And descant on mine own deformity.
>
> [I.i.24-27]

Richard determines to do evil, not because, like the Vice, his allegorical significance demands it, but because he has been "cheated of feature by dissembling nature" (l. 19). This psychological framework, as we have seen in *3 Henry VI*, stretches Shakespeare's conception of the role far beyond that of his sources, for whom Richard's deformity is merely emblematic, and far beyond the elementary characterization of the *Henry VI* plays (see above, pp. 69-70).

---

[4] For the stage history of the play, see C. B. Young's account in the Cambridge edition, pp. xlvi-lxi. Despite occasional forays into the original, Cibber's bastardized version of the play dominated the stage until Irving's productions in 1877 and 1896-97.
[5] P. 228.
[6] Pp. 386-407.

Richard III: The Self Alone

Despite the psychological complexity of Shakespeare's treatment of Richard, psychology alone offers an insufficient explanation of the character and his dramatic function, as many readers have realized. Hence the tendency among the more persuasive critics to describe, rather than explain, the character of Richard, to resort to metaphor as a means of suggesting both the underlying motives of the character and his dramatic effect. R. G. Moulton, for example, sees Richard as essentially an artist, driven by sheer intellectual enthusiasm to master and control the world around him; imperturbable, reckless, boldly imaginative, he is an "artist in villainy."[7] With a similar tendency toward descriptive analogy, A. P. Rossiter claims that Richard is above all an actor—"an actor consummate enough to make (quite literally) 'all the world a stage' and to work on humanity by the perfect simulation of every feeling...."[8] Though capturing much of the role's dramatic impact and providing a more satisfying rationale for the character's essential drives than the Renaissance commonplaces about ambition that are sometimes adduced to explain him, even these suggestive descriptions are somewhat misleading.[9] They explain, for one thing, very little of the role's significance. If Richard III's motivation is partially obscure, it is not because Shakespeare is exploring the abstruse psychology of the artist or actor but because what Richard means is at least as important as who or why he is. The role he plays, though vastly more complex than any in the *Henry VI* plays, is still translucent; one is still directed to look not only at but through it, to its underlying thematic origins. To neglect this level of meaning is to come dangerously close to reducing the play, as John Dover Wilson does, to melodrama.[10]

Shakespeare defines the essence of Richard's role in a scene of his own invention that, like others in the tetralogy, crystallizes in a striking dramatic image the central mode and meaning of the play. The emblematic function fulfilled in the *Henry VI* plays by the Countess of Auvergne episode, the "miracle" of Saint Albans, and Henry's "mole-hill" scene, is in *Richard III* fulfilled by the wooing of Anne. In contrast to these earlier emblematic scenes, the wooing of Anne is remarkable for the introduction of plausible

---

[7] *Shakespeare as a Dramatic Artist* (Oxford, 1893), p. 96.
[8] P. 16.
[9] For the motive of ambition see especially Ruth L. Anderson, "The Pattern of Behavior Culminating in *Macbeth*," *Studies in English Literature*, 3 (1963), 151-73, and Lily B. Campbell, *Shakespeare's 'Histories': Mirrors of Elizabethan Policy* (San Marino, Calif., 1947), pp. 308 ff.
[10] "The kind in question is not rightly tragedy, but melodrama; the melodrama of genius, yet all the more melodrama for that" (p. xl). To approach the play as tragedy is to impose upon it criteria of dubious relevance.

motivations: Richard's desire to make a politically advantageous marriage—presumably the "secret close intent / By marrying her which I must reach unto" (I.i.158-59)—and, more convincingly, his acute consciousness of deformity, which frames the action. The concluding soliloquy wittily reverses the complaint that opens the play:

> My dukedom to a beggarly denier,
> I do mistake my person all this while.
> Upon my life, she finds, although I cannot,
> Myself to be a marv'llous proper man.
> I'll be at charges for a looking-glass,
> And entertain a score or two of tailors
> To study fashions to adorn my body.
>
> [I.ii.251-57]

The political motive, however, is clearly of little consequence in this scene or elsewhere, and the psychological motive, though more apparent and more plausible, is itself problematic. To adopt a psychological reading of the scene, for example, demands an explanation not only of Richard's motives but of Anne's, a difficult task since the character is so briefly developed. The exaggerated artifice of the scene, moreover, suggests that its mode is more symbolic than psychological. The seduction of Anne provides the play's most shocking emblem of Richard's mysterious power, what Moulton calls a "secret force of irresistible will,"[11] and at the same time defines in precise dramatic terms the nature of the evil which that will brings into being.

At the very center of the scene, obviously enough, is the theme of love: Richard woos and wins his lady. The theme is articulated, however, in a subtler and richer manner than has usually been recognized. Throughout the exchange, two sets of love conventions are manipulated: the Petrarchan mode, familiar from earlier wooings in the series, and the Christian, introduced for the first time in Richard's repudiation of charity at the end of Part III (V.vi.81-83). The Petrarchan conventions are the more obvious and sustain the middle section of the scene; Richard's amorous rhetoric parodies the choplogic of the sonneteers. With neoplatonic ease he proves that Anne, not he, is guilty of the death of her husband and of the kingly father-in-law whose bier dominates the stage:

> Your beauty was the cause of that effect—
> Your beauty that did haunt me in my sleep
> To undertake the death of all the world
> So I might live one hour in your sweet bosom.
>
> [I.ii.121-24]

---

[11] P. 97.

Richard III: The Self Alone 79

Anne's beauty, not surprisingly, is Richard's "day," his "life," his "sun"; her eyes, which she wishes basilisks, might just as well be: "I would they were, that I might die at once; / For now they kill me with a living death" (ll. 151-52). From the use of such metaphors it is an easy leap to the reality of Richard's breast bared before the drawn sword; and from that to the dazzling non-sequitur, "Then bid me kill myself, and I will do it" (l. 186). After a fatal moment of indecision—"I would I knew thy heart" (l. 192)—Anne finally succumbs to the irresistible logic of the conventions Richard so guilefully controls: since she cannot bring herself to kill the man, it follows that she must love him. And the two break into iambic trimeters, a shift that signifies, as does the perfect sonnet woven by Romeo and Juliet, the conquest of love:[12]

Anne. I would I knew thy heart.
Glo. 'Tis figur'd in my tongue.
Anne. I fear me both are false.
Glo. Then never was man true.
Anne. Well, well, put up your sword.
Glo. Say, then, my peace is made.
Anne. That shalt thou know hereafter.
Glo. But shall I live in hope?
Anne. All men, I hope, live so.
Glo. Vouchsafe to wear this ring.
Anne. To take is not to give.
          [*Puts on the ring*]
                                    [I.ii.192-202]

The Petrarchism occupying the center of the episode is framed by another, more serious conception of love that resonates even more powerfully throughout the play and throughout the tetralogy as a whole. It is signaled at the opening of the scene by a series of puzzling but insistent allusions to Saint Paul. The first, spoken immediately before Richard's entrance, occurs in Anne's curiously specific reference that the corpse of Henry VI is being taken from Saint Paul's cathedral to be interred at Chertsey (I.ii.29-30). Upon his entrance Richard swears twice by Saint Paul within the space of eight lines, and in a context that bristles with Christian overtones. Anne's first words to Richard reproach him for having come "to stop devoted charitable deeds" (l. 35), and as she bids him begone, the language becomes overtly theological. "Sweet saint, for charity, be not so curst" (l. 49), Richard urges at first, and later, after the sight of Henry's bleeding corpse calls out from Anne a piercing cry of vengeance, "Lady, you know no rules of charity, / Which renders good for bad, blessings for curses" (ll.

---

[12] For the significance of the shift in verse pattern, see Whitaker, p. 70.

68-69). In opposing charity to vengeance, preaching the virtues of the new law over the old, Richard ironically lives up to the promise implicit in his oaths to Saint Paul. It is with a similarly Pauline appeal, in fact, that Richard completes his seduction, for as he places the ring on Anne's finger at the end of the episode, he pleads that she "leave these sad designs / To him that hath most cause to be a mourner" so that he may inter the dead king and "wet his grave with my repentant tears" (ll. 210-15). Anne accedes with her most compromising reply: "With all my heart; and much it joys me too / To see you are become so penitent" (ll. 219-20). It is one of the play's finer ironies that Richard turns even the better instincts of his natural opponents to his advantage.[13]

Hence the emblematic action of the scene: Richard, a Pauline Petrarch, inverting with insidious effectiveness the ideals of religious and romantic love. Although original in its details, the scene conflates motives expressed separately in soliloquies in Part III: the alienation from sexual love appears first in response to Edward's wooing of Elizabeth (III.ii) and the repudiation of charity upon the stabbing of Henry VI (V.vi). After the seduction of Anne, Richard's Petrarchan posturing is abandoned, and with it, except for tactical motives, the emphasis on his deformity. But the mockery of charity remains. The import of his actions is obvious enough: he murders his brother, his nephews, his wayward friends, his enemies; scorns his mother; drives wedges of hostility between the queen's kinsmen and his own. Richard is above all a violator of families, a destroyer of the last vestiges of communal ties remaining from the civil wars; one recalls the Judas kiss with which he greets the young prince at the end of *3 Henry VI*, an action signalizing the emergence of a new bond of loyalty, to the self alone. With the violation of charity in action comes the incessant mockery of words, as Richard chortles from one pious commonplace to another all the way to the throne. He pardons the murderers of Clarence, whoever they may be: "God pardon them that are the cause thereof!" (I.iii.315). He thanks God for his humility (II.i.72). He swears constantly by Saint Paul. He answers the vindictiveness of the gulls around him, he assures us, with true Christian forbearance:

---

[13] As John Dover Wilson notes in his introduction to the Cambridge edition, the oath "by Saint Paul" occurs only once in More's *History*, when Richard swears that he will not dine until he sees the head of Hastings, "in obvious allusion to *Acts* xxiii, which relates how forty Jews took an oath 'that they would neither eat nor drink till they had killed Paul'" (p. xx). It may be, as Wilson suggests, that Shakespeare "missed the original point" because he "was less familiar with the Scriptures" than More, but he surely creates from the oath his own scriptural resonances.

> But then I sigh, and with a piece of Scripture,
> Tell them that God bids us do good for evil.
> And thus I clothe my naked villainy
> With odd old ends stol'n forth of holy writ,
> And seem a saint when most I play the devil.
>
> [I.iii.334-38]

He accepts the crown with a final, extravagant gesture of piety, standing aloft, prayer book in hand, between two bishops—"two props of virtue for a Christian prince," Buckingham assures the Mayor, "to stay him from the fall of vanity" (III.vii.96-97).

If in subverting love Richard proves to be a descendant of the medieval Vice, as Bernard Spivack has demonstrated, his ancestry can be as easily traced through the *Henry VI* plays.[14] The Vice, indeed, provides a natural symbol of the inhuman and anarchic residue of the dissension those plays portray. As the eternal alien, the disrupter of all the bonds that delimit and define the human condition, the Vice demands little adjustment to become an embodiment of the accumulated perversions of civil war, less to become a reductio ad absurdum of the tendencies of the Yorkist family line. Richard's "I am myself alone," in fact, merely translates into "human" form a state of being which for the allegorical Vice is a necessary metaphysical condition. The progression of the Yorkist line, as we have seen, runs from the elder York, who, despite his violation of the bonds of loyalty to the throne, is restrained and humanized by deep familial love, to Edward and Clarence, who, although still sentimental about family ties, break them unblinkingly at moments of crisis for the sake of lust and injured pride; Richard, declaring "I have no brother," set apart from spiritual, romantic, and familial love, utterly amoral and alienated, steps outside the boundaries of humanity. And in doing so he becomes a kind of superman: his wit, his lucidity, his invulnerability, all derive, it seems, from his self-willed isolation. In naturalizing the Vice-figure, then, Shakespeare has adapted the allegorical alienation of the role to the moral and social alienation of the times he depicts; the Vice becomes an embodiment of the final stage of a long historical process.

The historicizing of the Vice adds to the role a new dimension, that of time. Although a temporal process invariably affects the fortunes of the Vice—the allegorical schema insures his ultimate defeat as certainly as history necessitates Richard's—Richard's relationship to time is considerably more complex. Ironically, Richard considers himself at the outset to be beyond the scope of

---

[14] Pp. 405-7.

history, free to shape the future in his own distorted self-image: "I am determined to prove a villain / And hate the idle pleasures of these days" (I.i.30-31). Indeed, his conquest of Anne, the woman whose father-in-law and husband he has murdered, is in part a triumph over the past:

> Hath she forgot already that brave prince,
> Edward, her lord, whom I, some three months since,
> Stabb'd in my angry mood at Tewksbury?
>
> [I.ii.239-41]

That one can erase the past, make oneself anew through sincere repentance, is ironically the burden of his appeals to Anne's Christian piety. Yet as we have seen from *3 Henry VI*, Richard is not free from history but is himself a symptom of its disordered state, an "unlick'd bear-whelp" of the civil wars. As the play unfolds, moreover, it becomes increasingly clear that Richard is not merely a product of the time but its chosen purge.

That Richard's role is conditioned by time becomes apparent with intensely ironic effect upon the first appearance of Margaret. As Richard taunts Queen Elizabeth and her kindred, the former queen, now a ghostly, brooding presence, enters unobserved and, in a series of asides, undermines his words:

Glo.	Poor Clarence did forsake his father, Warwick,
	Ay, and forswore himself—which Jesu pardon!—
Q. Mar.	Which God revenge!
Glo.	To fight on Edward's party for the crown;
	And for his meed, poor lord, he is mewed up.
	I would to God my heart were flint like Edward's,
	Or Edward's soft and pitiful like mine.
	I am too childish-foolish for this world.
Q. Mar.	Hie thee to hell for shame and leave this world,
	Thou cacodemon; there thy kingdom is.

[I.iii.134-44]

An ironic gap already exists between Richard and his audience by virtue of historical necessity. But with Margaret's unobserved entry there appears for the first time in the play a character whose level of awareness seems superior to Richard's. Once Margaret reveals her presence, of course, Richard demonstrates the supremacy of his wit, even to the extent of turning her curse against herself by inserting her own name at the appropriate moment:

Q. Mar.	. . . . .
	Thou slander of thy heavy mother's womb,
	Thou loathed issue of thy father's loins,
	Thou rag of honor, thou detested—

Richard III: The Self Alone 83

Glo. Margaret!

[I.iii.231-34]

One senses, however, that the exchange results in a standoff rather than a victory, that the time will come when Margaret's vision of the future will turn the last laugh against Richard:

> Stay, dog, for thou shalt hear me.
> If heaven have any grievous plague in store
> Exceeding those that I can wish upon thee,
> O, let them keep it till thy sins be ripe,
> And then hurl down their indignation
> On thee, the troubler of the poor world's peace!

[I.iii.216-21]

From this point on an aura of expectancy hangs over even Richard's most dazzling successes, clouding them with the certainty of his eventual doom.

Above all, Margaret's curses cause Richard's actions to become henceforth equivocal. While Richard bustles about undoing his enemies, he is at the same time destroying Margaret's. Clarence dies at Richard's command, yet Clarence is cursed by Margaret. And the same can be said of the rest of Richard's victims; Hastings, Rivers, Grey, Vaughan, the princes, Buckingham—all appear in Margaret's litanies, all except the princes recall her words as they meet their end. As each curse is fulfilled, it becomes increasingly clear that Richard is executing a will greater than his own (and too great to be Margaret's either), the will of Providence. The irony is a terrible one, for it means that Richard, the archindividualist, the archenemy of love, is not a "self alone" after all but the unknowing victim of a scheme of retribution neither he nor anyone else in the play seems able to control. It is this broad view of Richard's villainy that A. P. Rossiter invokes in his phrase "angel with horns";[15] chuckling all the while at his diabolical evil, yet ultimately as ineffectual as Satan himself, Richard unknowingly brings about good.

Although wittily appropriate, Rossiter's image, like Spivack's description of the Vice, ignores the play's vital and complex dimension of time. To do justice to this dimension, one must view Richard's role within a tradition of evil specifically temporal in orientation—that of the Antichrist. Richard's function as "angel with horns," after all, is defined in terms of the full sweep of historical process; like the Great Beast of the Apocalypse, he is not only a blasphemer and mocker of God but a depraved product of

---

[15] P. 20.

the time and the time's chosen scourge. In order to appreciate the manner in which such an archetype informs Richard's role, however, one must examine the extent to which the play as a whole is shaped by a conception of history that can justly be called apocalyptic.

That the world of the play is suffused with a distinctive sense of historical process can be best appreciated by means of a comparison with Shakespeare's chief source, More's *History of Richard III*. Juxtaposing the two works proves especially illuminating, since it offers a rare glimpse at Shakespeare's handling of a historical interpretation which, even in the slightly garbled versions of Hall and Holinshed, constitutes an artistic whole. More's *History* opens with a brief description of Edward IV and the state of the realm during the last years of his reign. Having given over the "fleshely wantonnes" of his youth, Edward has won the wholehearted affection of his people and created what can only be called a golden age: "And in his latter daies he left all wild daliaunce, and fell to gravitee, so that he brought his realme into a wealthie and prosperous estate, all feare of outwarde enemies were clerely extinguished, and no warre was in hande nor none towarde, but suche as no manne looked for. The people were towarde their prince not in a constrained feare, but in a true lovyng and wilfull obedience emongeste theim selfe, and the commons were in good peace." In an anecdote brilliantly evocative of the atmosphere of this idyllic time, More tells of an occasion the summer before Edward's death, when the king invited the mayor and aldermen of London "to hunte and make pastyme" with him at Windsor, "where he made theim not so hertye but so familiare and frendly chere, and sent also to their wives suche plenty of venison, that no one thyng in many daies before gatte hym either mo hartes or more hertie favour emongest the common people, which oftentymes more esteme and take for greate kyndenesse a little courtesie then a greate profite or benefite." This "love of his people and their entiere affection towarde hym," More regretfully concludes,

> had been to hys noble chyldren ... a mereveilous fortresse and a sure armoure, yf the division and dissencion of their frendes had not unarmed theim and left theim destitute, and the execrable desire of soveraiyntie provoked hym to their destruccion, whiche yf either kynde or kyndnesse had holden place must nedes have been their chiefe defence. For Richard duke of Gloucester, by nature their uncle, by office their protectoure, to their father greately beholden and too theim by othe and allegiaunce bounden, all the bandes broken and violated whiche bynde man and man together, withoute any respecte of God or the worlde, unnaturally contrived too bereve theim,

Richard III: The Self Alone

not onely of their dignitee and preheminence, but also of their naturall lives and worldely felicitee.

For More, then, Richard's overweening ambition interrupts a peaceful and ordered world, a peculiarly English Eden, composed of hunting and good cheer for commoner and king. As we have already observed (p. 72), Edward himself becomes on his deathbed the spokesman for the highest values of this world, warning his nobles against the "serpent" ambition—the Edenic overtones here reach their highest pitch—and pleading with them to join together in defense of the princes: "I exhorte and require you all, for the love that you have borne to me, and for the love that I have borne to you, and for the love that oure Lorde beareth to us all: From this tyme forward all greves forgotten, eche of you love other...."[16] Edward's eloquence fails, of course, but his character and the final years of his reign stand as symbols of the personal and public values Richard undermines. The image of a peaceful realm destroyed by the intrusion of the "serpent" ambition suggests classical as well as Christian precedents, moreover, which More as a humanistic historian is careful to include. The idealization of Edward's final years, as Richard S. Sylvester has shown, forms part of a complex of subtle echoes of Tacitus' account of Tiberius, who also transformed a world at peace into a reign of terror.[17] It is through such multiple allusions that More shapes the mere "history" of Richard's reign into a self-contained and timeless paradigm of the workings of tyranny.

Though no more "accurate" than More's, the backdrop Shakespeare creates for Richard's reign implies a radically different conception of history. In Shakespeare's version the twelve peaceful years of Edward's rule simply evaporate; Richard's opening soliloquy places the action of the play at a time immediately following the victory at Tewkesbury, which concludes Part III: "Now is the winter of our discontent / Made glorious summer by this sun of York...." The pressure of the past, indeed, is felt in every moment of the play: in the bleeding of Henry's corpse before Richard, in the painful memories of participants in the civil wars (or their forgetfulness, as in the case of Anne), above all in the interminable catalogs of Margaret, who hovers above the action like some inverted amnesiac, unable to for-

---

[16] *Hall's Chronicle* (London, 1809), pp. 345-46. For a thorough review of the sources behind the play, see *Narrative and Dramatic Sources of Shakespeare*, ed. Geoffrey Bullough, III (London, 1960), 221-48.

[17] *The History of King Richard III*, Yale Edition of the Complete Works of Saint Thomas More, ed. Richard S. Sylvester, II (New Haven, 1963), lxxxi (n. 4), xciii.

get. Edward's character, though not of paramount importance to the play, typifies the extent to which a distinctive historical consciousness seeps into all of its episodes. Unlike More, Shakespeare creates through the role of Edward a sense of continuity with the past at both the personal and political levels, a continuity that makes of his final years not an interval of peace and harmony in contrast to Richard's reign of terror but a fitting culmination of his own disordered youth and the moral chaos of the civil wars.

Edward does not enter the play until the beginning of Act II, his first appearance since the final scene in *3 Henry VI*, when he had announced with pathetic naiveté the onset of his "lasting joy." Now, sick and dying, he is brought in to the assembled nobles, as in More's account, to attempt a final reconciliation before being called to his maker. In both More and Shakespeare the scene is redolent of dissembled affection; as Hall describes it, "there in his presence (as by their woordes apeared) eche forgave other, and joyned their handes together, when as it after appeared by their dedes their hartes were far a sunder."[18] Shakespeare enlivens the irony with Richard's impish piety (and in this example with an image that betrays his sense of freedom from the past):

> I do not know that Englishman alive
> With whom my soul is any jot at odds
> More than the infant that is born to-night.
> I thank my God for my humility.
>
> [II.i.69-72]

Even more significantly, Shakespeare interrupts the family gathering with Richard's abrupt announcement of Clarence's death, news that whitens the faces of all present and profoundly unsettles the king: "Is Clarence dead? The order was reversed" (l. 86). When Lord Stanley enters to petition the king to pardon his servant for slaying a "riotous gentleman"—yet another addition to More—his request evokes from Edward a long reminiscence of his own and Clarence's past:

> Have I a tongue to doom my brother's death,
> And shall that tongue give pardon to a slave?
> My brother kill'd no man—his fault was thought,
> And yet his punishment was bitter death.
> Who sued to me for him? Who, in my wrath,
> Kneel'd at my feet, and bid me be advis'd?
> Who spoke of brotherhood? Who spoke of love?
> Who told me how the poor soul did forsake

---

[18]*Hall's Chronicle*, p. 345.

> The mighty Warwick and did fight for me?
> Who told me, in the field at Tewksbury
> When Oxford had me down, he rescued me
> And said "Dear Brother, live, and be a king"?
> Who told me, when we both lay in the field
> Frozen almost to death, how he did lap me
> Even in his garments, and did give himself,
> All thin and naked, to the numb cold night?
> All this from my remembrance brutish wrath
> Sinfully pluck'd, and not a man of you
> Had so much grace to put it in my mind.
>
> [II.i.102-20]

That this is a speech of remonstrance as well as self-reproach testifies to the subtlety of Shakespeare's resistance to More's idealization: having only moments before delivered a sermon on the virtues of forgiveness and love, Edward turns vindictive for a crime for which, as far as he knows, he is completely responsible. Like many of Richard's victims, Edward finally accepts his guilt but soothes his conscience with the perverse consolation that he will not suffer alone: "O God, I fear thy justice will take hold / On me, and you, and mine, and yours, for this!" (ll. 131-32). His words are echoed, significantly, not only by Richard, whose "God will revenge it" (l. 138) conveys a twofold irony, but by Clarence's son in the ensuing scene, only a moment before Queen Elizabeth announces Edward's death: "God will revenge it; whom I will importune / With earnest prayers all to that effect" (II.ii.14-15).

The dislocation caused by the announcement of Clarence's death thus turns much of the irony of the reconciliation scene against Edward himself. This is so not merely because the news creates an unflattering impression of the man whom More idealizes but because it exerts upon the present moment the pressure of the past. While striving to establish the groundwork for a peaceful future, for the "lasting joy" he looks forward to at the end of *3 Henry VI*, Edward becomes enmeshed in the web of time: first, by his startled recognition that his orders rescinding the murder of Clarence had not been carried out—itself an emblem of one's inability to erase the past—and then by the memories of his brother that flood his mind in painful detail as he grapples with the reality of his guilt. Shakespeare achieves these effects only by departing quite radically from his source, since according to More the murder had occurred (and been much lamented) a number of years prior to Edward's death.[19] At other moments in the play, moreover, Shakespeare adds further accusations from Edward's

---

[19] Ibid., p. 342.

past. "Though not by war, by surfeit die your king," exclaims Margaret, alluding to the "fleshely wantonnes" which, according to More, Edward abandoned as he aged (I.iii.97); the occasional innuendos concerning Jane Shore extend the implications of this charge. A more serious reminder of the past emerges at the end of the play in Margaret's final reference to the dead king: "Thy Edward he is dead, that killed my Edward" (IV.iv.63). Through all of these details—of complicity in the murder of Clarence and Prince Edward, of surfeiting and lechery—Shakespeare creates for Edward and the world he inhabits an inescapable sense of time. For Edward and most of those around him, history becomes, in Joyce's metaphor, a nightmare from which one cannot awaken. Indeed, in the dreams of Clarence and Richard, the play dramatizes that very image.

The most telling way in which Shakespeare alters the implications of his sources is through the inclusion of Margaret; having been banished to France upon Edward's accession, she appears in none of the accounts of the reign. Yet it is Margaret's presence that determines most profoundly the temporal orientation of the play, for it is through her prophecies that the crimes of the civil wars reach out to destroy the future. All who die at Richard's hands die within Margaret's historical frame. The retributive process she foresees has been described by many critics—its fearful symmetries are all too readily apparent—but an appreciation of its full significance requires at least some attention to detail. The execution of Hastings can be taken as a paradigm for all the rest, it seems, for although the names of the victims change, the rhythm of their downfalls scarcely varies, imparting to the majority the same degree of facelessness they achieve as counters in Margaret's periodic reckonings. Hastings's death too reveals a manipulation of the sources characteristic of the play as a whole and serves as yet another reminder that the play's pattern of history is woven not by the chroniclers but by Shakespeare himself.[20]

Margaret's malediction against all the Yorkists links Hastings with Rivers and Dorset:

> Rivers and Dorset, you were standers by,
> And so wast thou, Lord Hastings, when my son
> Was stabb'd with bloody daggers. God, I pray him,
> That none of you may live his natural age,
> But by some unlook'd accident cut off!
>
> [I.iii.210-14]

---

[20]Tillyard claims that "in *Richard III* Hall's pattern of history is there in its full seriousness" (p. 227).

Richard III: The Self Alone

Hastings appears as unmoved by this as all the others who are forced to endure Margaret's rhetorical onslaughts, and he is equally unperturbed later by the prophetic warning contained in Stanley's rather more precise vision: "this night / He dreamt the boar had razed off his helm" (III.ii.10-11). Instead of fleeing, Hastings attends the appointed meeting in the Tower, blithely secure in his belief that he is high in Richard's graces:

> I think there's never a man in Christendom
> Can lesser hide his love or hate than he;
> For by his face straight shall you know his heart.
> [III.iv.53-55]

In ringing Hastings's death with such weighty ironies, Shakespeare follows More, for whom the image of a man grotesquely unaware "that the axe hong so nere his awne head" exerted a peculiar fascination. But the tone of the two episodes differs radically, as do their moral implications. More perceives in Hastings's naiveté what might be called the irony of mutability. For him Hastings's sudden fall is emblematic of the foolishness of man's blind faith in the permanence of human affairs, his trust that he can be immune to the dizzying turns of Fortune's wheel:

> O lorde God the blyndnesse of our mortal nature, when he most feared, he was in moste suretye, and when he reconed hym self moste surest, he lost his lyfe, and that within two houres after. Thus ended this honorable man a good knight and gentle, of great aucthoritie with his prince, of livyng somwhat dissolute, playne and open to his enemy, and sure and secrete to hys frende, easy to begyle, as he that of good harte and courage foresawe no perilles, a lovyng man and passyng welbeloved, very faythfull and trustie ynough, but trustyng to muche was hys destruction as you maye perceyve.[21]

In Shakespeare's version Margaret's curse alters considerably the nature of the emblem. No longer at the mercy of mutability, Hastings is now the victim of a retributive (and therefore historical) scheme. That in stressing Hastings's complicity in the murder of Prince Edward Shakespeare ignores his own account of the deed in *3 Henry VI* suggests the importance of the play's retributive design.[22]

The sympathies generated by More are curiously lacking in Shakespeare's version of Hastings's downfall, not only because of

---

[21] *Hall's Chronicle*, pp. 361-62.

[22] Hall affirms Hastings's presence at the murder of the prince (p. 301); when recounting his execution, however, he follows More and therefore makes no connection between the two events. It is this kind of homogenization of previous accounts that makes it virtually impossible to speak meaningfully of a "pattern of history" in either Hall's chronicle or Holinshed's.

the new emphasis on moral guilt but because of the meanness of character with which it is coupled. The potential for sympathy is there, of course—Hastings is victimized for his refusal to support Richard's claim to the throne—but the feelings evoked by his misguided self-certainty come closer to malicious pleasure than anxious dread. He positively gloats over the imminent execution of his enemies:

> But I shall laugh at this a twelve month hence,
> That they which brought me in my master's hate,
> I live to look upon their tragedy.
>
> [III.ii.57-59]

Heady with success, Hastings anticipates gleefully triumphs yet to come: "Well, Catesby, ere a fortnight make me older, / I'll send some packing that yet think not on't" (ll. 60-61). As in his treatment of Edward, Shakespeare seems more concerned to forestall sympathy than to evoke it. Indeed, there is much in the portrait of Hastings that reminds one of Richard; in his arrogance, his ignorance of his impending downfall, his jovial viciousness, he becomes a kind of caricature of the man who destroys him. Even the desire to "send some packing" recalls Richard's earlier phrase, "Till George be pack'd with posthorse up to heaven" (I.i.146).

Shakespeare seals the ironies in Hastings's fall by interspersing between his gloating and his beheading the brief interlude of the executions at Pomfret. As his enemies go off to the block, they recall Margaret's curse; Rivers, indeed, looks forward with a most un-Christian consolation to the fulfillment of all its clauses:

> Then curs'd she Richard, then curs'd she Buckingham,
> Then curs'd she Hastings. O, remember, God,
> To hear her prayer for them, as now for us!
>
> [III.iii.17-19]

In the next scene Hastings himself is dead. The fates of Rivers, Grey, and Vaughan—in their anonymity the Rosencrantzes and Guildensterns of the play—offer an illuminating example of the dramatic and historical sleight-of-hand with which Shakespeare shapes even the most trivial details into a symmetrical pattern of retribution. Vaughan, although he suffers silently the effects of Margaret's curse, is not included in it until after his death, at the point of her recapitulation in Act IV; nowhere in the chronicles, moreover, is he even remotely connected to the murder of Prince Edward. Grey's presence, if one thinks about it (there is little encouragement) is even more puzzling. He too is omitted from Margaret's initial curse, in spite of the fact that it is he who recalls it; he too had no part in the murder of the prince. Instead, it is

Richard III: The Self Alone

Grey's half brother, Dorset, who is present at the deed in Hall's account and who is cursed by Margaret, as we have seen, as a "stander by."[23] Later in the play (IV.i.91) Dorset slips away to Richmond and is thenceforth forgotten. In effect, then, Grey is executed as a stand-in for his brother, whose absence would rupture the continuity of the retributive scheme. Rivers, the only one of the three who finds himself in Margaret's opening curse, is nonetheless equally innocent of any connection with the prince's murder. According to More, whose judgment reveals the extent of Shakespeare's departure from his sources in the interest of his larger historical pattern, all three men were beheaded "without other yearthly gylt, but onely that they were good men and true to the kyng and to nye to the quene...."[24]

In short, though the play is structured upon what seems to be a series of *de casibus* tragedies, the genre is reduced to a single dimension. There is little room in *Richard III*, for example, for the downfall of innocents. Of all of the victims in Margaret's balance sheets, only the young princes are blameless, and they, it seems, are sacrifices to the Deity whom Ralegh repeatedly invokes in *The History of the World*—the one who punishes sinful kings "in their Children for many generations."[25] There is also little room for chance, for the arbitrary and capricious goddess Fortuna, whose fickleness is so often responsible—in More, in the chronicles, in the *Mirror for Magistrates*—for the refrains of the *de casibus* lament. Instead, the wheels that carry Clarence, Hastings, Buckingham, and the rest to their dooms spin with the precision of cogs in a machine, turned by the rising and falling motion of Richard. From More to the *Mirror for Magistrates*, the sources behind the play shift continually in their attempts to explain the tragedies of the reign, stressing retributive justice or Fortune's wiles as each becomes appropriate. Of all the accounts of the reign, only Shakespeare's imposes upon the moral ambiguities of history a system of retribution. When Margaret comments on the rightness of Anne's suffering, she accomplishes metaphorically the very usurpation of Fortune by Justice that occurs in the world of the play: "Thus hath the course of justice whirl'd about, / And left thee but a very prey to time..." (IV.iv.105-6). In *Richard III* Fortune turns a wheel of Justice—and Time himself, in an equally unfamiliar role, devours only the guilty.

The grimness of the play's system of justice has been stressed rather often; that the system is Shakespeare's own has not been

---

[23] *Hall's Chronicle*, p. 301.
[24] Ibid., p. 364.
[25] Walter Ralegh, *The History of the World*, ed. C. A. Patrides (Philadelphia, 1971), p. 59.

stressed enough. Instead, critics have been prone to assume a dependence on the chronicles or the so-called Tudor myth, as if the play's peculiar providential design were as much a "given" of the history as Richard's deformity.[26] To perceive the uniqueness of this severe and abhorrent scheme is one thing, but to rationalize it, quite another. Recent criticism of the play, indeed, has been in large part an effort to pursue its dramatic effect and philosophical implications. One can search optimistically as Tillyard does for "hints of a divine purpose in the mass of vengeance" that dominates the play.[27] But critics more sensitive to the play's moral dynamics have found them so repugnant as to call into question the very orthodoxies they have been said to sustain. A. P. Rossiter, for example, finds that the "demonic appeal" of Richard, coupled with the repulsive system of "justice" against which he bends his will, creates in the play "relatives, ambiguities, irony" that tend to undermine the easy pieties of the Christian world view. "Do I need to insist," he asks, "that the coupling of 'Christian' and 'retribution' itself is a paradox? That the God of vengeance is *not* a Christian God; that his opposite is a God of mercy who has no representation in this play."[28] Nicholas Brooke extends Rossiter's line of thought to suggest that the play's pattern of retribution, instead of enhancing one's sense that justice is fulfilled, converts the audience to the side of Richard because he opposes it: "Within this gigantic machine of order there is no place for the human will; we are oppressed by the same sense of helplessness as can be induced by a rolling mill.... To be good, is to submit to the crushing weight; the only resistance possible is the way of deliberate evil." For Brooke, Richard becomes ultimately "Mankind"—"the human representative, bolder than ourselves, resisting oppression, and being destroyed. The world not only seems, but is, the poorer for his loss."[29]

Both of these critics are right, it seems to me, in responding with shock and dismay to the retributive scheme which the play implies is justice. They are short sighted, however, in finding no Christian tradition which can render that sense of anguish meaningful—which is not to say less shocking, less dismaying. In certain modes of Christianity the coupling of "Christian" and "retribution" is no paradox at all. Surely Ralegh felt himself the best of Christians as he demonstrated with mathematical precision

---

[26] See the previously quoted observation by Tillyard (n. 20); see also Rossiter, pp. 20-22.

[27] Tillyard, pp. 234-35. Tillyard takes solace in what he considers to be the charity and penitence of Richard's victims, most of whom display neither virtue.

[28] P. 22.

[29] P. 79.

Richard III: The Self Alone

in the Preface to *The History of the World* that in England, in France, in Spain, in all recorded history "GOD is every where the same GOD" and He "will not be mockt."[30] More relevant to the play's retributive design than Ralegh's vision of divine judgment, however, is that provided by the book of Revelation. As we have already observed, Richard's role in the play is broadly analogous to that of the Antichrist; he is not merely a figure of demonic evil who fulfills the will of God, an "angel with horns," but one who mocks, parodies, inverts all Christian values, and is called forth by the time's corruption to serve as its purge. And what is this world which gives birth to Richard but a world of such wholesale corruption that justice, terrible as it may be, becomes itself a kind of mercy?

In the light of the play's depiction of this guilt-ridden time, consider the signs that Archbishop Sandys saw around him in 1585 to suggest the imminence of the Last Judgment:

Charity, being unto other virtues as the moon in comparison of the rest of the stars, is also changed: her sweet and amiable nature is converted into more than savage barbarity: tender-hearted men are become bloody-minded: every man hunteth after his brother as after a prey: each degree is maliced and hated of other, the clergy of the laity, the shepherd of the sheep, the rich of the poor, yea, the man of the wife, the parents of the children, the master of the servants, all men of some, and some almost of all. The bond of peace, the link of love, that malicious enemy hath burst asunder. What shall I say? Surely all things do shew that the end of all things is at hand.[31]

Or consider John Dove's description of the sins of the current age in a sermon of 1594:

God may now repent him, as he did in the dayes of Noah, that hee made man uppon the earth, for the prophesie of Christ is fulfilled: *Charitie waxeth colde, iniquitie doth abound: faith is not found upon earth.* There is a ripeness of sinne, and what can bee expected but an harvest, that the Angell thrust his sharpe sickle on the earth and cutte downe the clusters of the Vineyard, and cast them into the great wine fatte of the wrath of God. Sinne is not now *Peccatum habitans,* but *regnans,* not making his abode with us, but

---

[30] Pp. 59, 67.

[31] *The Sermons of Edwin Sandys* (Cambridge, 1841), p. 364; Sandys' sermon, on Luke, XXI.25 ("Then there shall be signs in the sun . . .") was first published in 1585. Anxieties concerning the Apocalypse preyed on many minds during the 1580s and 1590s. The Reformation brought a vast body of religious literature attempting to prove that the Pope was Antichrist. Ernest L. Tuveson provides a useful survey of this material in *Millenium and Utopia* (Berkeley and Los Angeles, 1949), pp. 22-70. Also pertinent, though more difficult to substantiate because of censorship, are the prophecies of Regiomantus, which assigned the end of the world to the year 1588; for a description of their impact upon Western Europe during 1587-88, see Garrett Mattingly, *The Armada* (Boston, 1959), pp. 175-86.

raigning over us, it hath gotten a longer and larger jurisdiction over the world, than Julius Caesar had over the Senat, which obtained *Perpetuam Dictaturam*: An everlasting Dictatorship, the like not heard of before. . . . And which is more, they be *Clamantia peccata*, crying sinnes, because the crie of them ascendeth up into heaven, as did the bloud of Abell for vengeance against us. . . .

"When that time shall come," Dove continues, "it will be manifest to all the world, that iniquity hath got the upper hand, that nothing can then be expected, but fire and brimstone to raine from heaven as it did upon Sodom. . . ."[32] In neither of these sermons is there anything cheerful or consoling about the Christian vision, merely the positive insistence that, although it may be abhorrent from a human perspective, God's will is just: "He taketh no rewards: his sceptre is straight, his judgment righteous, his eye simple: he will not be entreated of the wicked, neither shew them any mercy. In that day every one of them shall receive justice and just punishment. These are his properties; and he changeth them not. He seeth all: he hath all power: he is a righteous judge of all, and over all for ever."[33]

No other play of Shakespeare's is so narrowly retributive as *Richard III*, then, because of this play's unique historical dimension. Unlike More, as we have seen, Shakespeare conceives of history as process and the time of *Richard III* as the culmination of decades of civil dissension and civil war. And it is just such a vision of historical process that the tradition of the Apocalypse affords:

> so shall the World go on,
> To good malignant, to bad men benign,
> Under her own weight groaning, till the day
> Appear of respiration to the just,
> And vengeance to the wicked. . . .
>
> [*Paradise Lost* XII.537-41]

I do not intend to suggest that *Richard III* is an allegory of the Apocalypse or that Richard's role can be explained solely in terms of the Antichrist; as I observed earlier, the play represents a complex assimilation of a variety of dramatic and historical traditions. It is not as allegory that the Apocalypse informs *Richard III* but as an underlying cultural myth, an archetypal

---

[32] *A Sermon Preached at Paul's Crosse . . . Intreating of the Second Coming of Christ and the Disclosing of the Antichrist* (London, 1594), B7^v-B8^v, C3^v.
[33] Sandys, pp. 354-55.

Richard III: The Self Alone

presence that joins the play's conception of time to the larger structures of Christian history.[34]

In a play that chronicles the rise of a tyrant, the scene of Richard's coronation, the very apex of his success, is curiously anticlimactic. Even as he ascends the throne Richard's thoughts turn not to the "golden time" he anticipated in Part III (III.ii.127) but to his own insecurity:

K. Rich. Stand all apart. Cousin of Buckingham!
Buck. My gracious sovereign?
K. Rich. Give me thy hand.
[*Here he ascendeth the throne. Sound*]

> Thus high, by thy advice
> And thy assistance, is King Richard seated.
> But shall we wear these glories for a day;
> Or shall they last, and we rejoice in them?
>
> [IV.ii.1-6]

Denied even the luxury of an instant's exultation, Richard must attend immediately, as the wheel of justice spins under him, to the problem of keeping his balance. The effect is one of deliberate anticlimax, analogous in inverted form to the moment in *Paradise Regained* when Christ, having been placed on the pinnacle by Satan, stands firm. In *Paradise Regained*, as Northrop Frye has observed, the image of Christ poised miraculously on the pinnacle suggests the mysterious fusion of powers that occurs when God's will and man's become one.[35] In Richard's case, the opposite impression is created; one has the feeling of a source of power being withdrawn, of a man becoming in his self-sufficiency an empty shell. As Richard retreats into his own anxieties, one recalls Margaret's injunction that heaven withhold its plagues until his sins be ripe. And as he probes Buckingham's mind with hesitant indirection, one detects the first stirrings of "the worm of conscience" that Margaret prophesied should "still be-gnaw [his] soul" (I.iii.221). Having failed to seduce Buckingham, Richard turns angrily aside and "gnaws his lip" (IV.ii.27).

The gnawing of the lip is included by Hall in his general description of Richard: "when he strode musing he would byte and chaw besely his nether lippe, as who sayd, that his fyerce nature in his cruell body alwaies chafed, sturred and was ever

---

[34] For a perceptive study of the play's conception of time, especially its apocalyptic overtones, see Tom F. Driver, *The Sense of History in Greek and Shakespearean Drama* (New York, 1960), pp. 87-105, esp. pp. 101-3.

[35] "The Typology of *Paradise Regained*," in *Milton's Epic Poetry*, ed. C. A. Patrides (Baltimore, 1967), pp. 317-18.

unquiete."³⁶ Like the oath to Saint Paul, however, the detail is extended by Shakespeare to create a unique set of ramifications. Throughout the play Richard appears often in the role of a human (or subhuman) counterpart to Margaret's devourer, Time. Warning Buckingham of "yonder dog," Margaret says, "Look when he fawns, he bites; and when he bites, / His venom tooth will rankle to the death" (I.iii.289-91). Young York remarks that his uncle "could gnaw a crust at two hours old" (II.iv.28). And in her great recapitulation Margaret praises God that "this carnal cur / Preys on the issue of his mother's body / And makes her pew-fellow with others' moan!" (IV.iv.56-58). Richard goes about his murders with considerable culinary gusto, linking them invariably with pleasures of the palate. Clarence is "frank'd up to fatting for his pains" (I.iii.314). As Hastings departs for his meeting in the Tower, Buckingham mutters in an aside that he will not only "stay dinner there," as he intends, but "supper too, although thou know'st it not" (III.ii.122-23). Richard prefaces his execution of Hastings with an appetizer of strawberries, refusing other sustenance until the deed is done: "Off with his head! Now by Saint Paul I swear / I will not dine until I see the same" (III.iv.78-79). The motif recurs once more as Richard sends Tyrrel off to murder the princes—"Come to me, Tyrrel, soon at after supper, / When thou shalt tell the process of their death" (IV.iii.31-32)—and climaxes in Richmond's urgent exhortation to his forces:

> The wretched, bloody, and usurping boar,
> That spoil'd your summer fields and fruitful vines,
> Swills your warm blood like wash, and makes his trough
> In your embowell'd bosoms—this foul swine
> Is now even in the centre of this isle. . . .
>
> [V.ii.7-11]

Not until the night before Bosworth does Richard, unsettled by his growing sense of doom, glutted with the blood of his land, finally lose his appetite: "I will not sup to-night" (V.iii.48). The origin of the motif, as we have seen, lies in the imagery of bestiality and cannibalism that pervades *3 Henry VI*, specifically in Clarence's reference to Richard's "bloody supper" in the Tower (V.v.83). In Ulysses' description of the nature of historical process in *Troilus and Cressida*, the imagery of devouring suggests not only the destruction of the world but the ultimate destruction of the self: appetite "Must make perforce an universal prey, / And last eat up himself" (I.iii.123-24). Hence the significance of Richard, as the time of his downfall approaches, gnawing his lip.

---

³⁶ *Hall's Chronicle*, p. 421.

Richard III: The Self Alone

From the moment of his coronation, then, Richard's destructive impulses turn inward. In effect, the play at this point begins to swing full circle, the wheel of justice spinning Richard with increasing momentum toward his destined end. In the coronation scene, indeed, it is as if the play has begun again and Richard is henceforth doomed to reenact his earlier triumphs, this time as self-parody. Having disposed of Anne, he prepares once more to go a-courting, but without his former gaiety:

> I must be married to my brother's daughter,
> Or else my kingdom stands on brittle glass.
> Murder her brothers, and then marry her!
> Uncertain way of gain! But I am in
> So far in blood that sin will pluck on sin.
>
> [IV.ii.62-66]

When Buckingham returns later in the same scene, he discovers Richard lost in thought, musing anxiously over prophecies that Richmond will soon be king, an attitude toward the supernatural that reverses the indifference he displayed earlier in undoing Clarence with a similar prediction. Later events accentuate one's sense of déjà vu. The wooing of Elizabeth, as has often been observed, stands in pale contrast to the earlier wooing of Anne, Richard having lost his verve and, as appears thereafter, the game as well. That Elizabeth grants her daughter's hand to Richmond casts ironic reflections on Richard's brittle contempt: "Relenting fool, and shallow, changing woman!" (IV.iv.431). As Margaret balances her accounts in Act IV, it becomes apparent that Richard's death—all that remains to fulfill her sense of symmetry—is near: "But at hand, at hand, / Ensues his piteous and unpitied end" (IV.iv.73-74). Perhaps the most powerful reenactment of an earlier episode, at least to an Elizabethan audience, occurs in Richard's final confrontation with his mother. Having been mocked in her original blessing of Richard in Act II, his mother now turns against him: "Bloody thou art; bloody will be thy end. / Shame serves thy life and doth thy death attend" (IV.iv.194-95). In comparison to a mother's curse, even Margaret's terrible maledictions seem insignificant.[37]

The sense of inevitability evoked by the play's symmetrical structure is heightened by Richard's new consciousness of time, a consciousness that appears first, rather cryptically, in the scene in which he rejects Buckingham. Distracted by his thoughts of the

---

[37] As Keith Thomas illustrates, the curse of a parent was of especial dread to Elizabethans and was felt to be especially effectual; see *Religion and the Decline of Magic* (London, 1971), pp. 505-6.

prophecies that Richmond will become king, he finally responds to Buckingham's uncertain queries with a befuddling nonsequitur:

Buck.	My lord—
K. Rich.	Ay, what's o'clock?
Buck.	I am thus bold to put your Grace in mind Of what you promis'd me.
K. Rich.	Well, but what's o'clock?
Buck.	Upon the stroke of ten.
K. Rich.	Well, let it strike.
Buck.	Why let it strike?
K. Rich.	Because that like a Jack thou keep'st the stroke Betwixt thy begging and my meditation. I am not in the giving vein to-day.

[IV.ii.112-20]

The motif appears once more at the climax of Richard's attempt to win the hand of Elizabeth. Striving without avail to find something to swear by that he has not wronged in the past—having stumbled from his crown, himself, the world, his father's death, God—he seizes desperately upon "the time to come." As Queen Elizabeth observes, however, this oath too can have no meaning:

> That thou hast wronged in the time o'erpast;
> For I myself have many tears to wash
> Hereafter time, for time past wrong'd by thee.
> The children live whose fathers thou hast slaughter'd,
> Ungovern'd youth, to wail it in their age;
> The parents live whose children thou hast butcher'd,
> Old barren plants, to wail it with their age.
> Swear not by time to come; for that thou hast
> Misus'd ere us'd, by times ill-us'd o'erpast.

[IV.iv.388-96]

Like his victims before him, Richard has destroyed the future in the past. As Bosworth draws near, moreover, Richard's anxiety about the course of time presses home with crushing weight. "Tell the clock there," he orders, as the hour strikes; "Give me a calendar. / Who saw the sun today?" (V.iii.276-77). The apocalyptic overtones are clear: "in those days, after that tribulation, the sunne shall waxe darke, and the moone shal not give her light" (Mark XIII.24).[38]

Time assumes its most menacing guise for Richard on the night before Bosworth. As he sleeps, the ghosts of all his murdered victims, from Prince Edward to Buckingham, appear before both

---

[38] All biblical quotations are from *The Geneva Bible: A Facsimile of the 1560 Edition*, ed. Lloyd E. Berry (Madison, Wisc., 1969).

him and Richmond, dispensing curses to the one, to the other, blessings. The visitation convinces Richard of the reality of providential history. The nature of his dream, with its combination of allegorical and psychological elements, suggests the doubleness of the forces undermining him. The dream is not strictly internalized, as is Clarence's, for Richmond stirs on stage with identical visions; in this sense, the presence of the spirits suggests divine intervention. But since the visions occur in sleep, and since Richard's response is depicted with great psychological plausibility, the dream suggests as well the promptings of the inward spirit, the gnawing of conscience that Margaret had earlier foreseen. Awakening from his dream, at "dead midnight," Richard at last experiences what it is to be a self alone:

> What do I fear? Myself? There's none else by.
> Richard loves Richard; that is, I am I.
> Is there a murderer here? No—yes, I am.
> Then fly. What, from myself? Great reason why—
> Lest I revenge. What, myself upon myself!
> Alack, I love myself. Wherefore? For any good
> That I myself have done unto myself?
> O, no! Alas, I rather hate myself
> For hateful deeds committed by myself!
> I am a villain; yet I lie, I am not.
> Fool, of thyself speak well. Fool, do not flatter.
> My conscience hath a thousand several tongues,
> And every tongue brings in a several tale,
> And every tale condemns me for a villain.
> [V.iii.182-95]

The impression created by this speech, quite literally, is of a man trying to pull himself together. Yet the self he strives to integrate—"I am I"—continually splits apart. Tormented by his conscience, Richard discovers that to pursue the doctrine of "I am myself alone" leads, in the word's most profound sense, to confusion. The oath with which he attempts to seduce Queen Elizabeth achieves at this point an unexpected fulfillment:

> As I intend to prosper and repent,
> So thrive I in my dangerous affairs
> Of hostile arms! Myself myself confound!
> [IV.iv.397-99]

With Richard's dream, then, the fundamental values of community that are articulated at the very beginning of the tetralogy reassert themselves, if only in negative terms. The aggressive egocentricity that gradually reduces the state to chaos ultimately destroys the self. Richard's very language recalls once more the hero who in *1 Henry VI* had given voice to the communal ideal that Richard's life has denied:

> By the apostle Paul, shadows to-night
> Have struck more terror to the soul of Richard
> Than can the substance of ten thousand soldiers
> Armed in proof and led by shallow Richmond.
>
> [V.iii.216-19]

In his startled discovery that the shadows of a spiritual reality he has never acknowledged exert more force than the substance of ten thousand soldiers, Richard achieves an insight that Talbot never doubted:

> No, no, I am but shadow of myself.
> You are deceiv'd, my substance is not here;
> For what you see is but the smallest part
> And least proportion of humanity.
>
> [*1 Henry VI* II.iii.50-54]

That Richard marks his new discovery of the superiority of spirit to flesh with an oath to the apostle Paul adds a final irony to his mockeries of the much abused saint.

   Although it signalizes his disintegration as a man, Richard's soliloquy jolts the audience into a totally new perspective on his character. Despite its homiletic underpinnings, the soliloquy is the first of Shakespeare's career to foreshadow the soul-searchings of Hamlet or Macbeth, which plunge the audience into the intimate revelations of tormented thought. In *Macbeth* the explorations of a divided self begun in Richard's speech span the entire play. The dramatic effect of this technique is obviously humanizing; no longer is the audience smirking in detached amusement and horror at Richard's wiles but actually experiencing his innermost thoughts. The soliloquy is humanizing in another, theological sense as well, for it opens to Richard the possibility of becoming fully human, of creating out of the rubble of his old self a new one. The sufferings of conscience, after all, though Margaret sees them solely as a form of punishment, afford the potentiality of grace, make possible the kind of self-reorientation Cardinal Wolsey experiences when he exclaims, "I feel my heart new open'd" (*Henry VIII* III.ii.366). In Richard's case such a possibility seems mainly theoretical, but the fact that it exists creates an added dimension to his suffering at the end of the play. For as he goes off to battle, Richard repudiates his conscience, committing the one unforgivable sin, and consigns his soul to hell:

> Let not our babbling dreams affright our souls;
> Conscience is but a word that cowards use,

Richard III: The Self Alone

> Devis'd at first to keep the strong in awe.
> Our strong arms be our conscience, swords our law.
> March on, join bravely, let us to it pell-mell;
> If not to heaven, then hand in hand to hell.
> [V.iii.308-13]

The prospect of Richard's entrance into the realm of humanity is thus raised only to vanish in a final and irrevocable act of will.

By its very nature, Richard's repudiation of conscience infuses Margaret's earlier vituperations with a new and almost literal validity. More than any other character, Margaret revels in images and allusions linking Richard to forces of demonic bestiality. At various times he is an "elvish-marked, abortive, rooting hog"; a "slave of nature" and "son of hell" (I.iii.229-30); a "cacodemon" whose "kingdom" is in hell (I.iii.144); a fawning dog whose "venom tooth will rankle to the death" (I.iii.291); a "hell-hound that doth hunt us all to death" (IV.iv.48); "hell's black intelligencer," a "factor to buy souls and send them thither"(IV.iv.71-73); and much else. That Margaret herself is a guiltridden old harpy cannot help but vitiate somewhat the force of these epithets. But when Richard turns against his conscience, he himself assigns them a new significance. As Richard's day of judgment draws near, moreover, the role of Margaret is increasingly usurped by Richmond, a man untainted, unequivocally ordained to free the time. For Richmond too Richard is a "wretched, bloody and usurping boar" (V.ii.7); and his triumphant exclamation on the battlefield echoes exactly Margaret's last wish: "God and your arms be prais'd, victorious friends; / The day is ours, the bloody dog is dead" (V.v.1-2). There is a final providential irony in the fact that Margaret is denied her greatest desire: "Cancel his bond of life, dear God, I pray, / That I may live and say, 'The dog is dead'" (IV.iv.77-78). Though Shakespeare's images for Richard's satanic bestiality are appropriately less garish and recondite than biblical descriptions of the Great Beast of the Apocalypse, with his seven heads and ten horns, their effect is clearly analogous. As he exhorts his troops, in fact, Richard himself provides the clearest evidence for Shakespeare's naturalization of the "great dragon" of Revelation (XII.9): "Our ancient word of courage, fair Saint George, / Inspire us with the spleen of fiery dragons!" (V.iii.349-50).

If Richard becomes by the end of the play an English Antichrist, Bosworth Field, of course, becomes Armageddon. And the resemblances are not fortuitous. It is this final battle that the audience has anticipated since the beginning of the play as the decisive moment at which the disordered world of the civil wars will be purged and renewed. It is toward this moment that time itself seems directed. As she first curses Richard, Margaret evokes a sense of this temporal process with strong apocalyptic overtones:

> If heaven have any grievous plague in store
> Exceeding those that I can wish upon thee,
> O let them keep it till thy sins be ripe,
> And then hurl down their indignation
> On thee, the troubler of the poor world's peace!
>
> [I.iii.217-21]

With the fulfillment of her curses against Richard's victims, she perceives the ripeness of the time: "So now prosperity begins to mellow / And drop into the rotten mouth of death" (IV.iv.1-2). Now, she senses, the moment of Richard's judgment has come:

> But at hand, at hand,
> Ensues his piteous and unpitied end.
> Earth gapes, hell burns, fiends roar, saints pray,
> To have him suddenly convey'd from hence.
>
> [IV.iv.73-76]

As with Margaret's descriptions of Richard, it is left to Richmond ultimately to validate her conception of time. Urging on his forces, he echoes Margaret's words and forges a closer link between Bosworth and Armageddon:

> In God's name cheerly on, courageous friends,
> To reap the harvest of perpetual peace
> By this one bloody trial of sharp war.
>
> [V.ii.14-16]

The imagery of harvesting is among the most powerful in Revelation: "And another Angel came out of the Temple, crying with a loude voyce to him that sate on the cloud, Thrust in thy sickle and reape: for the time is come to reape; for the harvest of the earth is ripe.... And the Angel thrust in his sharpe sickle on the earth, and cutte downe the vines of the vineyarde of the earth, and cast them into the great wine presse of the wrath of God" (XIV.15,19). Although Richmond's arrival surely does not represent the Second Coming or his betrothal the marriage of the Lamb, his role is in every respect that of an agent of God. That he is personally something of a "stick," as John Dover Wilson complains, may be true but is to be expected; as in the case of the victorious Malcolm in *Macbeth*, Shakespeare subordinates the hero's personality to his symbolic function.[39]

---

[39] Wilson, p. xliv.

Richard III: The Self Alone

One can conclude, then, that the vision of historical process underlying *Richard III* has strong but subtle ties to the orthodoxies of the Old and New Testament. The conception of history is indeed a grim one, as critics like Rossiter and Brooke have observed, calculated to send shudders of distaste through modern sensibilities. There is no reason to believe, however, that it did not send shudders into the souls of Shakespeare's contemporaries, not so much of distaste, perhaps, as of horror and dread. God's justice, after all, is not what men in their hearts have ever wanted, even though they must applaud it. It is not merely a failure to respond imaginatively to archaic modes of thought that afflicts some modern criticism of the play, however, but a failure to perceive the significance of its historical dimension. When Rossiter wittily analogizes the play's retributive schema to Newton's Third Law, for example—"'Action and reaction are equal and opposite'"[40]—he betrays a characteristic insensitivity to the importance of the play's temporal orientation. Finding in the play's vision of justice a pattern as symmetrical as Newton's, and therefore utterly alien to mature Shakespearean tragedy, Rossiter is forced to conclude that the very perfection of the scheme implies ironic ambiguities and ambivalences. But the process of judgment in *Richard III* cannot be universalized in such a manner and abstracted from the dimension of time. The entire tetralogy, as we have seen, is rigorously historical, and only in such terms can one perceive — though not enjoy—the appropriateness of the terrible symmetry with which it concludes. It is this vision of history as process that gives not only *Richard III* but the series as a whole its distinctive meaning and form.

[40] P. 2.

The Later Histories:
From History to Character

As I have tried to suggest by repeated allusions to the later histories, Shakespeare's second tetralogy provides in many respects an illuminating critical framework for the first. Both groups of plays share the distinctive political and patriotic concerns that set them apart from the comedies and tragedies, of course, but they are also joined, as we have seen, in a variety of more specific ways. The dialectical interplay between Lucy and Joan at Talbot's death looks forward to the opposition between Hotspur and Falstaff. The thematic transition from chivalry to law in *1* and *2 Henry VI* recurs in *1* and *2 Henry IV*. Henry VI's "providentialism" foreshadows Richard II's, as does Duke Humphrey's respect for law that of John of Gaunt. The plot structure of *2 Henry VI* anticipates that of *Richard II*. The imagery of bestiality that pervades *3 Henry VI* haunts Bolingbroke's tormented imagination as he conjures up a future ruled by his riotous son. There are thus strong continuities in Shakespeare's concerns as a historical dramatist, in characterization, theme, plot, and imagery. In important respects the later histories can be seen as subtler, more complex, more aesthetically coherent elaborations of dramatic techniques and political insights expressed in the first tetralogy.

But despite their many interrelationships, it is difficult to make meaningful comparisons between the two tetralogies. There are obvious reasons why this should be so. With the exception of *Richard II,* the second series abandons the tragic mode of the first for comedy and epic. The later plays, moreover, are in every respect superior, in intellectual discrimination, in characterization, in dramatic focus—above all, in poetic power. In subject matter the two groups of plays cover reigns totally unlike, each opening up distinctive political issues and dramatic potentialities. Indeed, the persistent variety of Shakespeare's art and its adaptiveness to every mode of human endeavor seem calculated to frustrate a comparative or developmental view of his dramatic achievement. In spite of these difficulties, however, it is possible to identify with at least some degree of precision a major shift in Shakespeare's use of history in the later histories—a reorientation with important consequences for the kind and quality of dramatic experience those plays afford.

The most distinctive feature of the first tetralogy, I have argued, is the sense of a historical continuum that informs it. From the disrupted funeral of Henry V to Bosworth Field, the plays trace the successive stages of England's social disintegration, the gradual dissolution of all communal ties. As each bond is violated, a new, less inclusive one is forged as society regroups, to be broken in its turn: chivalric communion gives way to the rule of law, law to kinship, kinship to self-love. Each stage of the process, as we have seen, is carefully defined in terms of thematic development and characterization, imagery and stage action. As the series unfolds, moreover, episodes and characters take on an almost typological density—cross-references and repetitions (even verbal echoes) defining their significance in relation to times past and to come. With the emergence of Richard III, himself a symbol of the accumulated crimes of generations, the process of destruction gains momentum until the Armageddon of Bosworth Field. Controlling the dramatic experience of the first tetralogy, in short, is a fully articulated conception of historical process.

A kind of historical continuity is manifested in the second tetralogy as well. Although more clearly self-contained than the plays in the early series, the later histories are also bound together by interlocking characters and episodes. Family lines, in particular, are developed with a remarkable sense of continuity. The greater psychological depth in characterization contributes to a display of the biographical intricacies of the past far more detailed than anything in the earlier plays: "Jack Falstaff, now Sir John," Justice Shallow informs us in *2 Henry IV,* was once "a boy, and page to Thomas Mowbray, Duke of Norfolk" (III.ii.24-25). In a broader vein, the second tetralogy reverses the process depicted in the first. While the *Henry VI* plays articulate the gradual disintegration of an ordered society, ending in the apocalyptic reign of Richard III, the *Henry IV* plays portray the reintegration of a society disordered by rebellion and civil war, culminating in the heroic reign of Henry V. To characterize this development, Shakespeare turns, as in *Richard III,* to an underlying cultural myth.

As John of Gaunt makes clear, the world that is lost in *Richard II* is Eden:

> This royal throne of kings, this scept'red isle,
> This earth of majesty, this seat of Mars,
> This other Eden, demi-paradise . . .
>
> [II.i.40-42]

It is in an emblematic garden scene, which marks the transition from Richard's misrule to Bolingbroke's, that one finds the play's most unequivocal judgment of Richard as king:

> O, what pity is it
> That he had not so trimm'd and dress'd his land
> As we this garden!
>
> [III.iv.55-57]

The queen herself betrays with unconscious irony the role that Richard fulfills in the play's political mythology as she rebukes the gardener for speaking of his deposition:

> Thou, old Adam's likeness set to dress this garden,
> How dares thy harsh rude tongue sound this unpleasing news?
> What Eve, what serpent, hath suggested thee
> To make a second fall of cursed man?
> Why dost thou say King Richard is depos'd?
>
> [III.iv.73-77]

If England is Eden, then Richard's identity is not in question. He considers himself on occasion a Christly victim, but Adam too was Christ-like before altering forever the course of history. The curse Richard brings upon England, aided by Bolingbroke, is the curse of living in a fallen world—a world disordered by rebellion, ruled by an illegitimate monarch haunted by guilt and the threat of civil war.

When Hal banishes Falstaff at the end of *2 Henry IV*, this fallen world is reordered. Though there is room for much disagreement on the implications of this renewal, as the history of Shakespearean criticism suggests, there is no disputing it as a fact: in the typology of the plays, Hal's role is that of the second Adam, "redeeming time when men think least I will" (*1 Henry IV* I.ii.212). It is a role in which the errors of the first Adam are overturned, much to the amazement of Bolingbroke, who can see in his son only the old follies of Richard II reborn:

> For all the world
> As thou art to this hour was Richard then
> When I from France set foot at Ravenspurgh . . .
>
> [*1 Henry IV* III.ii.93-95]

The need to redeem the time grows particularly acute in Part II, as the social and political disorder set in motion by Richard's abuses and Bolingbroke's usurpation gathers momentum—seems destined, as Bolingbroke fears, to destroy the realm. From king to commoner England is sick, literally as well as figuratively, the time corrupted and diseased. Bolingbroke himself is mournfully aware

The Later Histories

of the realm's decay, though of too limited a moral sensibility to appreciate the ironies that shimmer on the surface of his diagnosis:

> Then you perceive the body of our kingdom
> How foul it is, what rank diseases grow,
> And with what danger, near the heart of it.
>
> [III.i.38-40]

Oppressed by age, illness, the betrayal of youthful expectations, the figures in this world feel themselves victims of time, driven on against their will to destinies over which they have no control. If he had been able to read the book of fate, Bolingbroke laments, he would have chosen death:

> how chance's mocks
> And changes fill the cup of alteration
> With divers liquors! O, if this were seen,
> The happiest youth, viewing his progress through,
> What perils past, what crosses to ensue,
> Would shut the book and sit him down and die.
>
> [III.i.51-56]

The rebels too are plagued by the pressure of past events, as their spokesman, the archbishop, complains to Prince John:

> The time misorder'd doth, in common sense,
> Crowd us and crush us to this monstrous form
> To hold our safety up.
>
> [IV.ii.33-35]

Even Falstaff, who in Part I seemed outside the rule of time—"What a devil hast thou to do with the time of day?" asks Hal in their first encounter (I.ii.6-7)—now feels the threat of its power, though admitting it only in moments of intimate self-revelation: "Peace, good Doll, do not speak like a death's-head, do not bid me remember mine end" (II.iv.231-32). Throughout the play, at both the political and private levels, one feels a sense of the inexorability of decay comparable to that which holds sway in the first tetralogy. There are hints in *2 Henry IV*, however, that history can be redirected, that the realm, as Westmoreland suggests, can still be cured:

> It is but as a body yet distemper'd,
> Which to his former strength may be restor'd
> With good advice and little medicine.
>
> [III.i.41-43]

In the redemption of Hal, Westmoreland's prognosis is vindicated. For Hal not only comes to terms with time but paradoxically reverses it, establishing the conditions for a second Eden. In doing so, he violates almost magically the natural course of time and the expectations built upon it:

> And Princes all, believe me, I beseech you,
> My father is gone wild into his grave,
> For in his tomb lie my affections;
> And with his spirits sadly I survive
> To mock the expectation of the world,
> To frustrate prophecies, and to raze out
> Rotten opinion, who hath writ me down
> After my seeming.
>
> [V.ii.122-29]

The marvel of Hal's emergence as national hero is that he halts what to all others seems an irreversible process of social and personal decay. Falstaff, above all, whose hopes are based upon the predictability of Hal's behavior, cannot cope with such a reversal. The result is that the moment which promises redemption for England proves for Falstaff a Last Judgment. Hal's startled words of admonition as he is interrupted in the midst of his coronation procession are thus appropriately (if unconsciously) scriptural: "I know thee not, old man. Fall to thy prayers" (V.v.47). Although Falstaff may have little else in common with the foolish virgins of the New Testament, to whom the line alludes, he does share their poor sense of timing. Like them, he has neglected to prepare for the coming of the master, in spite of repeated warnings. Like them, he is denied entrance to the festivities: "Afterwardes came also the other virgins, saying, Lord, Lord, open to us. But he answered, and said, Verely I say unto you, I knowe you not. Watche therefore: for ye knowe nether the day, nor the houre, when the Sonne of man wil come" (Matthew XXV.11-13). Having redeemed both himself and the time, Hal moves on to the conquest of France, an event that returns to England's possession a realm described in the Epilogue to *Henry V* as "the world's best garden."

Although a hasty survey can scarcely suggest the full implications of this underlying historical myth, it can serve as an indication, at least, of Shakespeare's continuing concern for the broad patterns of historical process. In comparison to the patterns of the first tetralogy, however, those of the second are only vaguely defined—not articulations so much as intimations of a historical dimension to experience—and curiously tangential to the major preoccupations of the plays. Instead of being at the center of attention, as in the *Henry VI* plays, a sense of history hovers on the fringes of events, evoked in passing allusions but subordinated to other interests. One's diminished awareness of history in the

The Later Histories

second tetralogy is prompted in part, no doubt, by the simple fact that little time passes. From the opening of *Richard II* to the conclusion of *Henry V,* after all, a mere seventeen years elapses, whereas the period contained by the first tetralogy spans sixty-three of perhaps the most chaotic years in English history. In the second tetralogy, history becomes to a very great extent biography—a study of Henry V as prince and king. Hence the de-emphasis on historical process is in one sense a function of Shakespeare's chosen medium.

There are signs, however, that the shift away from history is largely self-imposed and that neither the brevity of the historical period nor the focus on biography can completely account for it. Perhaps the most striking are the numerous inconsistencies between Parts I and II of *Henry IV,* inconsistencies far more obtrusive than any to be found in the earlier tetralogy. In Part I, for example, Hal breaks away from the world of the taverns, reconciles himself with his father, and triumphs over Hotspur at Shrewsbury to emerge, finally, a true chivalric hero. Yet in Part II he is once more in the taverns, full of regret for his wasteful life, unreconciled with his father, unthought of at court; once more he must win the favor of his father and astonish the world with his virtues. As Harold Jenkins has demonstrated, events in *2 Henry IV* clearly depend upon Part I in certain respects—the anticipated banishment of Falstaff, for example—but the play as a whole proceeds as if the main event in Part I, Hal's redemption, had never occurred. It is not that Hal has relapsed in Part II—that would be explicable in biographical terms—but that history has actually been erased; no one in the play is conscious of Hal's former redemption. "In the two parts of *Henry IV,*" Jenkins concludes, "there are not two princely reformations but two versions of a single reformation. And they are mutually exclusive." One can argue, of course, that in performance or in the reading such inconsistencies pass virtually unnoticed, so subtle is Shakespeare's sleight-of-hand. But this is exactly the point. To be unconcerned with such discrepancies, one must be experiencing the plays not as history or even biography but as some other mode. "The one thing about history," observes Jenkins, "is that it does not repeat itself"; one genre that does, he goes on to suggest, is folklore, a mode in which a hero "can be at the same point twice."[1] The same can be said of allegory, I would add; both literary forms are significantly ahistorical.

---

[1] *The Structural Problem in Shakespeare's* Henry the Fourth (London, 1956), pp. 24-25.

To address the issue of historical consciousness from another angle, we may compare the concluding plays of the two tetralogies. *Richard III*, as we have seen, is a work in which every episode is suffused with the presence of the past; Bosworth Field is the logical culmination not merely of Richard's reign but of the whole process of social dissolution that spans the tetralogy. *Henry V*, in contrast, is remarkably self-contained. The victory at Agincourt, of course, is not a natural culmination of forces set in motion in the reign of Richard II and cannot be celebrated as such; Hal's emergence as epic hero is not a fulfillment of historical process but an astonishing violation of its normal course. That such violations can be treated historically, however, is evident from the intimations of Hal's role as second Adam in the *Henry IV* plays; in Christian history, after all, there are antitypes as well as types. Yet there is little sense of such a continuum in *Henry V*. Even when Canterbury hints at a theological framework for Hal's reformation—"Consideration like an angel came, / And whipp'd th'offending Adam out of him" (I.i.28-29)—Ely's reply channels the remark into strictly biographical areas:

> And so the prince obscur'd his contemplation
> Under the veil of wildness; which, no doubt,
> Grew like the summer grass, fastest by night,
> Unseen, yet crescive in his faculty.
>
> [I.i.63-66]

The past figures on several other occasions, as in Falstaff's death of a broken heart or Henry's prayer before Agincourt, but its significance is invariably biographical.

Henry's prayer, in fact, offers an illuminating contrast to *Richard III*. It is the one moment in the play that recalls the usurpation of Bolingbroke:

> Not to-day, O Lord!
> O not to-day, think not upon the fault
> My father made in compassing the crown!
>
> [IV.i.298-300]

The dramatic thrust of this brief moment of anxiety suggests the degree to which history is underplayed throughout the second tetralogy. There is a faint tinge of irony in the lines, a hint that there will be turmoil under Henry VI, that second Edens cannot escape the taint of original sin. Yet the irony is subdued and subordinated to the conflict within Henry himself; psychology, not history, dominates the scene. Henry's recollection of the past, an act which in *Richard III* would have been fraught with ominous providential meaning, is personally, rather than historically, significant. History, in other words, has become internalized, psychologically defined, its objective dimension—dominant in *Richard III*—nearly swallowed up by the subjective dimension of personal memory. It is as memory that history exerts its pressure in the second tetralogy, especially in *2 Henry IV*, where the recollections of individuals, often distorted, often at odds, become one of the chief means of conveying a sense of the passage of time. Memory figures largely in *Richard III* as well, of course—witness Edward IV's moving reminiscences of Clarence's past acts of brotherhood—but in that play psychological pressures are invariably overshadowed by the ironic presence of an objective providential order. In *Richard III*, unlike *Henry V*, one's perception of the present moment is filtered through the continuum of time.

In certain respects this shift in perspective can be explained as a shift from a providential to a secular conception of history. John F. Danby sees evidence of such a transition as far back as *King John*: "The great change is the acceptance of history as a process not controlled by God, nor subject to the scheme of His revenges."[2] When compared to *Richard III*, *King John* and *Henry V* seem to offer striking evidence in support of this view. But this very fact calls attention to its limitations. For *Richard III*, as we have seen, embodies a providential conception of history precisely because of its position as the apocalyptic conclusion to the social disintegration depicted in the first tetralogy. No other play, before or after *Richard III*, exhibits so systematic a vision of divine purpose in history. Providential judgments exist in the *Henry VI* plays, as in the deaths of Suffolk and Winchester, but such judgments can hardly be said to constitute a providential interpretation of history; even the victory at Agincourt, after all, is not without providential implications. In general, the providential overtones in the early plays are less complex, less ambiguous, less realistically defined than those in the mature histories, but neither tetralogy embodies consistently a providential or secular conception. In both groups of plays both perspectives coexist—sometimes in a state of mutual support, sometimes in a state of tension. Neither early nor late in his career does Shakespeare compartmentalize experience in the manner that Danby suggests. As the unity of the first tetralogy makes clear, moreover, a conception of historical process need not depend on an exclusively providential interpretation of history.

---

[2] *Shakespeare's Doctrine of Nature* (London, 1948), p. 69.

A more convincing explanation of the second tetralogy's de-emphasis on history is suggested by the discrepancies in Parts I and II of *Henry IV*. Hal's mysterious "double reformation," as we have seen, violates history, violates biography. Yet it quite clearly serves a variety of dramatic functions. Most importantly, it enables Shakespeare to articulate in depth the virtues necessary to the role of an exemplary ruler. In the *Henry VI* plays, as we have seen, the themes of chivalry and law are exploited as a means of defining stages in a historical sequence; with their reappearance in the *Henry IV* plays, however, they serve to define, without reference to time, a single personality. As has often been observed, the *Henry IV* plays are structured upon an elaborate system of contrasts that defines the prince as a mean between undesirable extremes. A similar conception of political virtue underlies Elyot's attempt to construct the personality of an ideal governor. Indeed, Elyot's definition of the virtue of fortitude bears a remarkable resemblance to the distinctions drawn among Hal, Hotspur, and Falstaff:

> It is to be noted that to him that is a governor of a public weal belongeth a double governance, that is to say, an interior or inward governance, and an exterior or outward governance. The first is of his affects and passions, which do inhabit within his soul, and be subjects to reason. The second is of his children, his servants, and other subjects to his authority. To the one and the other is required the virtue moral called fortitude, which as much as it is a virtue is a mediocrity or mean between two extremities, the one in surplusage, the other in lack. The surplusage is called audacity, the lack timorosity or fear. I name that audacity which is an excessive and inordinate trust to escape all dangers, and causeth a man to do such acts as are not to be jeoparded. Timorosity is as well when a man feareth such things as be not to be feared, as also when he feareth things to be feared more than needeth.... And like as an excellent physician cureth most dangerous diseases and deadly wounds, so doth a man that is valiant advance himself as invincible in things that do seem most terrible, not unadvisedly, and as it were in a beastly rage, but of a gentle courage, and with premeditation, either by victory or by death, winning honour and perpetual memory, the just reward of their virtue.[3]

If applied directly to the characters of *1 Henry IV*, of course, Elyot's bloodless abstractions tend to reduce them to the scale of caricatures; Shakespeare has endowed his "types" with a life and liveliness that stretches their allegorical framework to the breaking point. Nonetheless, it is Hal's exemplary role as a mean between extremes that determines the structure of both parts of *Henry IV* and accounts for Shakespeare's departures from history. The

---

[3] *The Governor*, ed. S. E. Lehmberg (London, 1962), pp. 183-84.

The Later Histories

depiction of historical process, then, is subordinated to the depiction of character—not merely the individual psychologies of Hal, Hotspur, or Falstaff, though these take on a life of their own, but the generalized character of an ideal prince and king.[4] The dialectical mode of both plays creates for Hal a dimension outside the realm of time.

Although *Henry V* is based upon an epic structure, the effect on characterization is much the same. Critics may dispute the extent to which Shakespeare idealizes his portrait of Henry, but there is no arguing that it is the heroic tradition against which he is judged. As J. H. Walter has shown, each episode of the play serves as a touchstone for the conventional qualities of heroic kingship.[5] One sees Henry in council, in negotiations with foreign ambassadors, in prayer, in love—above all, in the varied postures of war. The method precludes the possibility of a developmental approach to character; instead of changing as the play unfolds, Henry's nature is revealed facet by facet as each episode calls forth an as yet untested quality of heroic leadership. In *Henry V* historical process is subordinated not to an allegorical mode but to epic convention, which makes of every episode a unique challenge and of Henry himself a paradigm—perfect or not—of epic kingship. That Shakespeare encountered in Holinshed's *Chronicles* a Henry V who "both lived and died a paterne in princehood, a lode-starre in honour, and mirrour of magnificence"[6] suggests that an exploration of heroic personality was not entirely a matter of choice. In reality, however, the path had been charted earlier in *King John*, a work which so clearly occupies a pivotal position between the two tetralogies that it demands careful consideration.

King John is Shakespeare's first political play. Unlike the earlier histories, which exploit political relationships as a means of defining stages in a historical process, *King John* exploits history as a means of posing and resolving dramatically a specific political problem. Not part of a tetralogy, the play is wholly self-contained, its issues and personalities isolated by definition from the continuities of historical development. As Adrien Bonjour has demonstrated, the work is structured upon the contrasted evolution of the two dominant characters, the Bastard Falconbridge and King

---

[4] For a discussion of the manner in which Hal synthesizes and rises above all three roles, see Fredson T. Bowers, "Theme and Structure in *King Henry IV*, Part I," in *The Drama of the Renaissance: Essays for Leicester Bradner*, ed. Elmer M. Blistein (Providence, 1970), pp. 42-68.

[5] See his introduction to the Arden edition of the play (London, 1954), pp. xiv-xvii.

[6] Quoted in *Narrative and Dramatic Sources of Shakespeare*, ed. Geoffrey Bullough, IV (London, 1962), 408.

John.[7] That they are thematic as well as psychological foils is established brilliantly in the play's opening scene.

The episode begins with John challenged by the French ambassador, Chatillon, to cede his throne to the rightful heir, Prince Arthur. John refuses to yield, however, and declares his readiness to invade France; he will stand firm, as he informs his mother, for his "strong possession" and his "right" (I.i.39).[8] As Eleanor privately assures him, however, it is the former rather than the latter ground that provides the sole basis for his authority:

> Your strong possession much more than your right,
> Or else it must go wrong with you and me:
> So much my conscience whispers in your ear,
> Which none but heaven, and you, and I, shall hear.
>
> [I.i.40-43]

In denying John's right to the throne, Shakespeare departs radically from accounts in the chronicles and from the source play, the *Troublesome Reign*. The scene continues with another violation of history, the entrance of the Bastard Falconbridge, a character with only the most shadowy of historical precedents in John's reign and others.[9] With the Bastard's arrival, dramatic attention centers once more on a dispute concerning the relative merits of possession and right, though this time in a private, rather than political, context. Confronted with the charge of bastardy levied by his younger brother, Robert, who has his father's will to support him, Falconbridge at first refuses to yield; as a son born in wedlock, he cannot be legally disinherited. That he is supported in his defense by John is not without irony, for as we discover later (II.i.192), his own claim rests upon a will of Richard Coeur de Lion that violates Arthur's rights of inheritance. Unlike John, the Bastard willingly forgoes his claim; when offered a position at court, he accepts immediately, declares his illegitimacy, and commits himself with gleeful abandon to the pursuit of honor:

> Brother by th'mother's side, give me your hand:
> My father gave me honour, yours gave land.
> Now blessed be the hour, by night or day,
> When I was got, Sir Robert was away!
>
> [I.i.163-66]

---

[7] "The Road to Swinstead Abbey: A Study of the Sense and Structure of *King John*," *ELH*, 18 (1951), 253-74.

[8] All citations to *King John* are from the Arden edition of E. A. J. Honigmann (London, 1954).

[9] The Bastard appears in the *Troublesome Reign* but in a version that bears little resemblance to Shakespeare's. For a useful account of the sources, see Bullough, pp. 1-24.

The Later Histories 115

Both John and the Bastard, then, are faced initially with a challenge to their legitimacy. Yet here the resemblance ends. John, by laying claim to a throne not rightfully his, places himself in a position of dubious moral and political authority, while Falconbridge, by accepting his bastardy and waiving a title that is legally (if not quite ethically) his, assumes the potential for a new legitimacy won in the pursuit of honor. The contrast between the spurious authority of a usurper and a youth who recklessly abandons the security of his position and aspires to honor reappears, in a somewhat different guise, in the *Henry IV* plays.

John's decision to hold fast to the crown has disastrous consequences for him and for England. Although a powerful and aggressive leader—he is in France with his troops before the French ambassador can gasp out his message to King Philip—John's every act is tainted by his false position. Even his eloquent refusal to bow to the authority of the Pope generates unexpected ironies: "What earthy name to interrogatories / Can taste the free breath of a sacred king?" (III.i.73-74) he demands of the papal legate. The pressure of events, moreover, soon ensnares John in the baleful logic of his usurpation. It is his victory against the French, paradoxically, which insures his downfall, for with Arthur in his possession he cannot resist the impulse to destroy him. As the papal legate quite shrewdly perceives, John's initial choice leads almost inexorably to further abuses:

> A sceptre snatch'd with an unruly hand
> Must be as boisterously maintain'd as gain'd;
> And he that stands upon a slipp'ry place
> Makes nice of no vild hold to stay him up:
> That John may stand, then, Arthur needs must fall;
> So be it, for it cannot but be so.
> [III.iii.135-40]

With Arthur's death John's authority collapses: the nobles rebel in protest and join forces with the French invasion. In the face of the chaotic swirl of events that overtakes him—a foreign invasion, a rebellion, the death of his mother—John becomes utterly unnerved, at the mercy of his own anxieties and the papal legate he had originally treated with contempt. A moral and political cripple, he abandons his responsibilities to Falconbridge: "Have thou the ordering of this present time" (V.i.77). He dies consumed by a poison that seems spiritual as well as physical in origin:

> Within me is a hell; and there the poison
> Is as a fiend confin'd to tyrannize
> On unreprievable condemned blood.
> [V.vii.46-48]

In the context of John's betrayal of his and the realm's moral integrity, the final words of the play suggest a deeper, more insidious danger to a king or kingdom than mere rebellion: "Nought shall make us rue / If England to itself do rest but true!"

While John's choice leads inexorably to moral and political bankruptcy, the Bastard's provides the freedom for self-determination. John ends a spiritual and physical ruin, the Bastard a national hero. Yet the Bastard's role is at first clouded with moral ambiguities. In part these are created by the sheer force of dramatic convention; royal sire notwithstanding, Falconbridge is still a bastard, a fact that was bound to excite in an Elizabethan audience at least suspicions of moral degeneracy. Indeed, Shakespeare plays on the convention by deliberately juxtaposing bastardy with usurpation. Inevitably suspect as well are the vital, almost anarchic energies he embodies and the cynical thrust of his wit; there is more than a touch of Richard III in the role, in fact, though the more extravagant dimensions of Richard are toned down by a new naturalness in characterization. Like Richard, the Bastard is automatically an outcast from society, the bar sinister serving almost as effectively as the hump as a badge of social alienation. Like Richard, too, he finds his vantage point uniquely liberating—offering not only a keen ironic perspective on the follies and foibles of the world around him, but the ability to turn those practices to Machiavellian advantage: "Since kings break faith upon commodity, / Gain, be my lord, for I will worship thee!" (II.i.597-98). Social detachment in both cases breeds a vigorous assertion of individualism, though the Bastard's "I am I, howe'er I was begot" (I.i.175) is admittedly somewhat less radical in its sense of isolation than Richard's "I am myself alone." Unlike Richard, the Bastard reverses rather than fulfills the conventional expectations created by his role: he wins his legitimacy.

The Bastard's career, like John's, reaches a turning point with the death of Arthur. As John F. Danby observes, the Bastard's response to this event constitutes a remarkable moment in Shakespeare's development as a political dramatist. As he watches the nobles defect to the French in protest against the apparent political murder of the prince, Falconbridge first directs Hubert to carry off the corpse, then, while waiting, grapples with the disastrous implications of the event:

> I am amaz'd, methinks, and lose my way
> Among the thorns and dangers of this world.
> How easy dost thou take all England up
> From forth this morsel of dead royalty!
> The life, the right and truth of all this realm

The Later Histories

> Is fled to heaven; and England now is left
> To tug and scamble, and to part by th'teeth
> The unow'd interest of proud swelling state.
> Now for the bare-pick'd bone of majesty
> Doth dogged war bristle his angry crest
> And snarleth in the gentle eyes of peace:
> Now powers from home and discontents at home
> Meet in one line; and vast confusion waits,
> As doth a raven on a sick-fall'n beast,
> The imminent decay of wrested pomp.
> Now happy he whose cloak and ceinture can
> Hold out this tempest. Bear away that child
> And follow me with speed: I'll to the king.
> A thousand businesses are brief in hand,
> And heaven itself doth frown upon the land.
> [IV.iii.140-59]

In a fluid and colloquial verse of great poetic urgency, the speech expresses the mental turmoil of a character as he confronts a crisis that puts to the test all his political and moral faculties. The lines begin in amazement and end in action.

Danby, whose appreciation of the dramatic significance of this moment is quite keen, finds in the Bastard's concluding affirmation of loyalty to King John a "really 'blind' patriotism—a feeling for 'England right or wrong.' "[10] For Danby the speech is one in which chauvinism is elevated as a political ideal—an ideal Shakespeare proceeds to celebrate in the second tetralogy through the character of Prince Hal. Needless to say, Danby's argument issues in a severe criticism of the political ideology underlying the later histories. There is no question that the new sense of commitment the Bastard discovers within himself at this moment is patriotic in nature; his first act is to go to the king. Yet there is (or has been, historically) a difference between patriotism and chauvinism, and there is nothing in the Bastard's speech to suggest the latter. Indeed, the focal point of the scene lies in a contrast between the blindness of the nobles, who react with a moral outrage that Danby presumably condones, and the clear-sightedness of Falconbridge. Although the moral sensitivity of the nobles is admirable in itself—Shakespeare comes closer to justifying their rebellion than any other in the histories—it is coupled with a political naiveté that nearly ends in their own and the realm's undoing; the French, who welcome them with open arms, are at the same time preparing to betray them when the war is won. Unlike the nobles, the Bastard responds to Arthur's death with cautious skepticism, a

[10] P. 78.

response ironically aided by his ignorance; having had no advance warning of John's intentions, he is better able to trust Hubert's truthful protestations of innocence. But as his response reveals, his suspicions run deep; he must act upon the assumption that political treachery has been committed, that the political and moral integrity of the realm has been irreparably destroyed. Although profoundly shaken by this newest application of the doctrine of commodity, and dreading its consequences, he reacts not with blind moral outrage but with anguished circumspection. Loyal to the ideal of England though fearing the reality, he will weather out the storm. Unlike Henry VI, whose demands for complete moral purity prove only debilitating, the Bastard achieves the insight that even in a fallen world one must act. From this point on, he becomes the voice and arm of England. Unable to incite the distraught John to political action, he accepts the "ordering of the time" and leads the English forces against the French. It is he who makes the play's concluding gestures of political loyalty, by kneeling before the new English king and by giving voice to the reasoned patriotism his actions embody: "Nought shall make us rue / If England to itself do rest but true."

In the Bastard Falconbridge, then, Shakespeare creates a character whose development weds the "politic" insights and energies of Richard III and the lesser machiavels of the *Henry VI* plays—Suffolk, Winchester, York—to the moral commitment of a Talbot or a Gloucester. A similar ideal is implicit in the earlier plays—Gloucester's combination of quick-wittedness and unswerving loyalty comes near to embodying it—but only in *King John* does it receive full dramatic articulation. Figures like Talbot and Gloucester, although they partially realize this ideal, fulfill significantly different roles. Conceived in terms of historical process, their personalities are restricted within the dimension of time, subordinated to the developing pattern of the tetralogy as a whole. Because of this they exist primarily as representatives of a single ideal—chivalry or justice—rather than as unified personalities who combine in their natures the varied attributes necessary for effective rule. In *King John,* in other words, the limiting frames of historical and thematic development give way to considerations timeless and universal in their scope. If the Bastard emerges as a figure right for the ordering of the time, it is not merely because he exemplifies a particular virtue demanded in the reign of King John, but because the fullness of his capacities makes of him a man for all seasons. With the creation of the Bastard, then, Shakespeare moves from history to character. And his drama is the richer for it.

The Later Histories

That the nature of political personality dominates Shakespeare's imagination in the histories after *King John* is evident in the extent to which the Bastard prefigures Prince Hal. Like Hal, Falconbridge is a composite creation, a character who on occasion threatens to split apart into the lesser roles he contains within him. In the conception of the Bastard, in fact, are integrated two roles that emerge in *1 Henry IV* as full-blown personalities—those of Hotspur and Falstaff. The presence of Hotspur shadows the Bastard on numerous occasions. Both characters share the gambler's impulse to hazard all in the pursuit of glory, no matter what the cost—"Brother, take you my land, I'll take my chance" (*King John* I.i.151)—and a bloodthirsty exuberance at the prospect of war that seems its natural corollary:

> Why stand these royal fronts amazed thus?
> Cry "havoc!" kings; back to the stained field,
> You equal potents, fiery kindled spirits!
> Then let confusion of one part confirm
> The other's peace; till then, blows, blood, and death!
>
> [*King John* II.i.355-60]

Coupled with the relish for blows is a contempt for words—especially the oily rhetoric of political intrigue. Whether it be Hubert's attempt to save Angiers by the main force of language or Lewis's "politic" appeals for the hand of Blanche (II.i), the Bastard responds with scornful impatience to all action merely verbal. To Lewis's glibness he reacts with an antipetrarchan outburst suggestive of Hotspur's attitude toward his wife. "Drawn in the flattering table of her eye!" he snorts, echoing Lewis's conceit:

> Hang'd in the frowning wrinkle of her brow!
> And quarter'd in her heart! he doth espy
>   Himself love's traitor: this is pity now,
> That hang'd and drawn and quarter'd, there should be
> In such a love so vile a lout as he!
>
> [II.i.504-9]

When the Bastard himself tries his hand at such stratagems, his device is anything but indirect (he exhorts the French and English to level Angiers together and then get on with the war), as is the mockery that goes with it: "How like you this wild counsel, mighty states? / Smacks it not something of the policy?" (II.i.395-96). Contemptuous of the niceties of politics or courtship, full of bluster and braggadocio in the pursuit of honor, the Bastard swaggers through court and battlefield as if he were Hotspur's country cousin.

Paradoxically, elements in the Bastard's character appear later in Falstaff as well, many of them transmitted through the Bastard from Richard III and the Vice traditions behind him. Like Falstaff, the Bastard is a man of wit—a quality Hotspur reveals only when he pauses in his hot pursuit of honor to mock the pretensions of courtiers or to tease his wife. By contrast, the Bastard has a jest for all occasions, an ebullience of epic dimensions. He breezes into the royal presence with a dazzling indifference to courtly etiquette:

> If old Sir Robert did beget us both
> And were our father, and this son like him,
> O old Sir Robert, father, on my knee
> I give heaven thanks I was not like to thee!
>
> [I.i.80-83]

At this point Queen Eleanor detects charming echoes of Coeur de Lion in the Bastard's spirit and John applauds him as a "good, blunt fellow" (l. 71), but there are times when such outspoken irreverence must sort ill with politics. After Constance concludes her harangue against Austria for betraying Arthur, for example, the Bastard pricks him repeatedly with her parting taunt, only to be silenced by the king:

> *Aust.*   O, that a man should speak those words to me!
> *Bast.*   And hang a calve's-skin on those recreant limbs.
> *Aust.*   Thou dar'st not say so, villain, for thy life.
> *Bast.*   And hang a calve's-skin on those recreant limbs.
> *K. John.*   We like not this; thou dost forget thyself.
>
> [III.i.56-60]

At this point quips must not be permitted to upset the delicate balance of commodity that keeps peace among the ruling powers. Even in war, as Falstaff learns at Shrewsbury, wit can be an offense to majesty. "I protest / I have not sought the day of this dislike," exclaims Worcester in defense of his rebellion:

> *King.*   You have not sought it? How comes it, then?
> *Falstaff.*   Rebellion lay in his way, and he found it.
> *Prince.*   Peace, chewet, peace!
>
> [*1 Henry IV* V.i.25-29]

When the Bastard discovers that the world spins on an axis of commodity, he achieves an insight recognizably Falstaffian—one the fat knight acquired at birth, no doubt, along with his white head and round belly; it is Falstaff, however, not Falconbridge, who acts upon the Bastard's conclusion: "Gain, be my lord, for I will worship thee!" (II.i.598). Although not prone to idolatry of

The Later Histories 121

any sort, Falstaff would not miss advancement if it lay in his path: "I would to God," he sighs to Hal, "thou and I knew where a commodity of good names were to be bought" (II.ii.85-87). Hence the Bastard's wit, his social and self-detachment, his initial moral ambiguity—all subdued inheritances from Richard III—eventually work their way into the character of Falstaff.

That Falconbridge's personality combines elements of Hotspur and Falstaff suggests the nature of his kinship with Hal. Although the Bastard's attributes are fleshed out to become full personalities in *Henry IV,* they retain at one level their former identity as components of a single self. In the psychomachia of the play, Hal must not only defeat his two foils but hold in precarious balance some of their virtues. At a more literal level, moreover, Hal's career in Part I parallels very closely the Bastard's. Something of a madcap at first, he too discovers at a moment of crisis—again, a rebellion—a new sense of commitment and maturity of purpose; he too is faced with the prospect of sustaining a throne collapsing under the moral and political strain of usurpation. As the Bastard emerges fully mature and takes upon himself the ordering of the time, his very accents anticipate the distinctive tonality of Hal as prince and king. Consider, for example, the rhetorical flamboyance of the Bastard's vaunt before the combined forces of the French and the rebellious nobles:

> Shall that victorious hand be feebled here,
> That in your chambers gave you chastisement?
> No: know the gallant monarch is in arms
> And like an eagle o'er his aery towers,
> To souse annoyance that comes near his nest.
> And you degenerate, you ingrate revolts,
> You bloody Neroes, ripping up the womb
> Of your dear mother England, blush for shame:
> For your own ladies and pale-visag'd maids
> Like Amazons come tripping after drums,
> Their thimbles into armed gauntlets change,
> Their needl's to lances, and their gentle hearts
> To fierce and bloody inclination.
>
> [V.ii.146-58]

As both Lewis and the Bastard are aware, the speech is nine-tenths braggadocio, but it is braggadocio redeemed by the exigencies of the occasion and by the self-consciousness of wit—"Their thimbles into armed gauntlets change." It is the tension between passionate national commitment and the detached awareness implied by wit that imparts to the Bastard's speech a vital integrity quite unlike the rhetorical subterfuges of Lewis, say, or Hubert before Angiers. The dauntlessness of Hotspur, the shrewd playfulness of Falstaff, are here conjoined in the service of the nation. The synthesis of energies is uniquely Shakespearean, it seems, having no precedent in the customary handbooks for princes. Although there is no single speech in *Henry IV* or *Henry V* that strikes quite the same note as this, one recalls Hal's witticism in the very act of rejecting Falstaff (*2 Henry IV* V.v.52-55) or Henry's bombast before Harfleur (*Henry V* III.iii), which achieves a bloodless victory for his sick and weary soldiers.

The Bastard Falconbridge, then, the first major character in the histories to have no basis in the chronicles, represents Shakespeare's first attempt to explore the means by which political legitimacy may emerge from a fallen world. That the problem is articulated in terms of the emergence of a heroic personality is a natural consequence of the shift from history to politics characteristic of the play as a whole. For in nearly all Renaissance political thought—in Erasmus's *Education of a Christian Prince*, in Machiavelli's *Prince*, in Elyot's *Governor*, in Castiglione's *Courtier*—it is the question of character that forms the basis for all political discourse. The underlying premise that unites these works, despite radical differences on many issues, is that a well-ordered commonweal depends upon the control of a well-ordered mind. "It is to be noted," writes Elyot, in the passage previously discussed, "that to him that is a governor of a public weal belongeth a double governance, that is to say, an interior or inward governance, and an exterior or outward governance. The first is of his affects and passions, which do inhabit within his soul, and be subjects to reason. The second is of his children, his servants, and other subjects to his authority." Implicit in Shakespeare's continuing exploration of the kingly personality in the plays from *Richard II* to *Henry V* is the assumption that the basis of all political order lies in the "inward governance" of the ruler.

In *Richard II* the extent to which Shakespeare probes the unsettling personal and political consequences of this assumption is readily apparent. It is apparent as well, though in a subtler vein, in the radical differences in treatment afforded such similar characters as the Bastard Falconbridge and Prince Hal. In *King John* the Bastard sustains the role of kingly prototype as a unified character who matures and develops throughout the course of the play. In the *Henry IV* plays, however, the biographical impulses so consistently pursued in *King John* are deflected by the inconsistencies in Hal's double reformation, and the role itself is splintered into the separate personalities of Hal, Falstaff, and Hotspur. With the increasing complexity of the forces demanding

The Later Histories

to be balanced by the heroic personality of the prince, moreover, comes an increasing subtlety and volatility in their interaction. Not only must Hal assimilate some of the attributes of Hotspur and Falstaff; he must dissociate himself from others in gestures of renunciation never required of the Bastard. Not only must Hal's courage be differentiated from Hotspur's audacity; his betrayal of Falstaff's expectations must be distinguished from his brother John's betrayal of the rebels.

From this perspective the most telling moment in the *Henry IV* plays occurs when Hal, at the moment of rejecting Falstaff, relapses into wordplay:

> Make less thy body hence, and more thy grace;
> Leave gormandizing; know the grave doth gape
> For thee thrice wider than for other men.
> Reply not to me with a fool-born jest;
> Presume not that I am the thing I was;
> For God doth know, so shall the world perceive,
> That I have turn'd away my former self;
> So will I those that kept me company.
>
> [*2 Henry IV* V.iv.52-59]

"Reply not to me with a fool-born jest"—the admonition stops Falstaff short, prevents him from using the reference to his girth to insinuate himself once more into his former role. But the warning occurs only after Hal has first checked himself, has recognized sharply that he cannot afford to lapse into his old habits, linguistic or otherwise; it thus suggests that the cost of kingship consists in a severe self-restraint and self-control. In order to govern a kingdom, one must first rule the mind. The final moments of *King John*, in which the Bastard kneels before his future king, imply the successful integration of private desires and political responsibilities; the final scene of *2 Henry IV*, however, dramatizes the necessity of choice and the narrowing of options that choice inevitably entails. Hal must subordinate himself to his office, must subject his happier impulses to rational self-control. In *2 Henry IV*, unlike *King John*, personal and political maturity carry with them a sense of loss.

It is this "inward governance" of the mind that constitutes the essence of heroic kingship in *Henry V*. From the council scene to the wooing of Kate, the major episodes of the play center upon the testing of Henry's capacity for self-mastery—heroism being defined as mental rather than physical action. The scene in which Henry confronts his treacherous nobles, for example, dramatizes a pattern of response typical of the play as a whole. Infuriated not only by their betrayal but by their callous indifference to their guilt, Henry bursts into a passionate denunciation of their crime. The full force of his indignation explodes upon his childhood comrade, Lord Scroop:

> But O,
> What shall I say to thee, Lord Scroop? thou cruel,
> Ingrateful, savage and inhuman creature!
> Thou that didst bear the key of all my counsels,
> That knew'st the very bottom of my soul,
> That almost might'st have coin'd me into gold
> Would'st thou have practis'd on me for thy use,
> May it be possible that foreign hire
> Could out of thee extract one spark of evil
> That might annoy my finger?
>
> [II.ii.93-102]

The emotions that inform this speech—shock, rage, grief, even a hint of vindictiveness—generate a compelling impression of Henry's full humanity; as he himself expresses it elsewhere, "in his nakedness" a king "appears but a man" (IV.i.106). Yet scarcely moments after this outburst Henry has risen above all personal feeling and levies upon the traitors an impartial, emotionless judgment:

> Touching our person seek we no revenge;
> But we our kingdom's safety must so tender,
> Whose ruin you have sought, that to her laws
> We do deliver you.
>
> [II.ii.174-77]

To find in Henry's treatment of the nobles a manner "somewhat priggish if not heartless," as Robert Ornstein does, is to ignore the emotional and dramatic movement of the scene.[11] The measured judgment that follows upon Henry's passion marks a heroic exercise of self-restraint. Ornstein's response, however, pinpoints one of the major problems in Shakespeare's handling of the epic mode throughout the play. This situation, like many others, implies inner conflict, yet Shakespeare so enshrouds Henry in his public role that conflict is allowed scarcely more articulation than a tightening of the lip. The true drama of the play, it seems, lies within Henry, in areas of feeling which, except for a few moments the night before Agincourt, remain submerged beneath a public facade.

That Shakespeare sensed more than dramatic limitations in the heroic mode of *Henry V* is suggested by the fact that his next (or

---

[11]*A Kingdom for a Stage* (Cambridge, Mass., 1972), p. 187.

perhaps concurrent) portrait of the rational man is that of Brutus in *Julius Caesar*. For in the character of Brutus the problem of ordering the mind for the public good is given tragic development. Like Henry V, Brutus strives to put service to the state above self-interest; like Henry, Brutus is forced to choose between friendship and duty. In the case of Brutus, however, the audience is not excluded from crucial moments of mental conflict; instead, one is drawn into the confused workings of a mind at war with itself:

> Between the acting of a dreadful thing
> And the first motion, all the interim is
> Like a phantasma, or a hideous dream:
> The genius and the mortal instruments
> Are then in council; and the state of man,
> Like to a little kingdom, suffers then
> The nature of an insurrection.
>
> [II.i.63-69][12]

In *Julius Caesar* the perception that political order demands mental order is pursued to tragic conclusions: out of Brutus's internal insurrection springs the chaos of civil war. Antony's final eulogy of Brutus as a paradigm of temperance thus stands in part as an ironic reminder of a noble man's incapacity to order his own mind:

> This was the noblest Roman of them all.
> All the conspirators save only he
> Did that they did in envy of great Caesar;
> He only, in a general honest thought
> And common good to all, made one of them.
> His life was gentle, and the elements
> So mix'd in him, that Nature might stand up
> And say to all the world, "This was a man!"
>
> [V.v.68-75]

The passage serves as a fitting end, it seems, not only for Brutus but for Shakespeare's explorations of political personality throughout *King John* and the second tetralogy. For with the shift from the England of Henry V to the Rome of Julius Caesar, Shakespeare moves away from the distinctive concerns of the English histories. In the tragedies that follow not only is the historical continuum subordinated to politics, but politics itself recedes before the universals of the human condition and man's radical imperfection.

---

[12] The citations to *Julius Caesar* are from the Arden edition of T.S. Dorsch (London, 1955).

Index

Index

Alexander, Peter, xin
Amyot, Jacques, 40
Anderson, Ruth, L., 77n

Bacon, Francis, 70
Berman, Ronald S., 58n, 62, 74n
Bevington, David M., 2n
Bonjour, Adrien, 113
Bowers, Fredson T., 37n, 113n
Brockbank, J. P., 1, 60, 64
Brooke, Nicholas, 75n, 92, 103
Bullough, Geoffrey, 26-27, 85n, 114n
Burckhardt, Sigurd, 2n

Calderwood, James L., 48n
Campbell, Lily B., 77n
Castiglione, Baldassare, 122
Chapman, George, 21-23, 29
Cicero, 59, 62
Clemen, Wolfgang, 75n

Danby, John F., 111, 116-7
Doran, Madeleine, xin
Dove, John, 93-94
Driver, Tom F., 95n

Edward III, 4
Elyot, Sir Thomas, 30, 38, 40, 45, 49n, 63, 112, 122
Erasmus, Desiderius, 50n, 122

Fiedler, Leslie A., 17-18
Foxe, John, 36-37
French, A. L., 12
Frye, Northrop, 95

Gorboduc, 58
Gordon, D. J., 22-23
Greene, Robert, 3-4

Hall, Edward, 11, 29, 58, 84, 86, 89n, 91
Henslowe, Philip, xii
Holinshed, Raphael, 11, 60, 84, 89n, 113

Homily against Disobedience and Wilful Rebellion, 58
Hooker, Richard, 29-30, 48-49, 62
Hunter, G. K., 9

Jenkins, Harold, 109
Johnson, Samuel, 16n, 20, 42, 53

Kelly, Henry A., 11
Kelso, Ruth, 37n
Kirschbaum, Leo, xin

Machiavelli, Niccolò, 40-41, 122
Malone, Edmond, xin
Manheim, Michael, 49n-50n
Mattingly, Garrett, 93n
Milton, John: *Paradise Lost*, 94; *Paradise Regained*, 95
Mirror For Magistrates, 91
More, Sir Thomas, 64-65, 69-70, 72, 75-76, 84-89, 91, 94
Moulton, R. G., 77-78

Nashe, Thomas, 16

Ornstein, Robert, 31n, 41n, 69, 124

Pearce, J., 18n
Peele, George, 25-26
Powell, Jocelyn, 9n
Price, Hereward T., 22-23
Price, Martin, 19

Ralegh, Sir Walter, 91, 92-93
Reese, M. M., 1-2, 11n, 68-69
Ribner, Irving, 4n, 11n
Ricks, Don, M., 29n, 58n
Riggs, David, 1, 10n
Rossiter, A. P., 27, 39, 75n, 77, 83, 92, 92n, 103

Sandys, Edwin, 93, 94n
Seneca, 75

Sidney, Sir Philip, 25-26, 37
Spenser, Edmund, 25
Spivack, Bernard, 76, 81, 83
Sylvester, Richard S., 85

Thomas, Keith, 13n, 97n
Tillyard, E. M. W., 2, 11-13, 43, 75-76, 92
Troublesome Reign of John King of England, The, 114
Tuveson, Ernest L., 93n

Walter, J. H., 113
Whitaker, Virgil K., 75n, 79n
Wilson, John Dover, xin, 52n, 77, 80n, 102
Woodstock, 27, 39-40

Yates, Frances A., 25-26
Young, C. B., 76n

OHIO UNIVERSITY LIBRARY

Please return this book as soon as you have finished with it. In order to avoid a fine it must be returned by the latest date stamped below.

JUL 13 1981 MAY 19 1989 OCT 22 2003

JUL 13 1981

JUL 27 1981

JUL 24 1981 JUN 6 1989

RETURN BY   RETURN BY

MAR 4 1985 FEB 26 1990

QUARTER LOAN

MAR 21 1985

JUN 14 1992

RETURN BY MAY 17 1992

NOV 03 2003

JUN 1 1986

JUN 1 1986

RETURN BY

FEB 25 1987
FEB 23 1987

RETURN BY

CF APR 22 1988

APR 17 1988